Clutter-
FREE
Christianity

What God *Really*
Desires for You

Clutter-FREE Christianity

What God *Really* Desires for You

Robert Jeffress

WaterBrook
PRESS

CLUTTER-FREE CHRISTIANITY

Trade Paperback ISBN 978-1-4000-7092-3
eBook ISBN 978-0-30744-658-9

Published in the United States by WaterBrook, an imprint of the Crown Publishing Group, a division of Penguin Random House LLC, New York.

WATERBROOK® and its deer colophon are registered trademarks of Penguin Random House LLC.

Library of Congress Cataloging-in-Publication Data
Jeffress, Robert, 1955–
    Clutter-free Christianity : what God really desires for you / Robert Jeffress. — 1st ed.
        p. cm.
Includes bibliographical references.
    ISBN 978-1-4000-7092-3
    1. Christian life. 2. Simplicity—Religious aspects—Christianity. I. Title.
    BV4501.3.J435 2009
    248.4—dc22

                                 2008044726

Printed in the United States of America
2019

10 9 8 7

• • • • •

To Andy and Joan Horner,
two of God's most faithful servant-leaders
who model in every area of their lives
what it means to be a follower of Jesus Christ.
Thank you for being such an encouragement to your pastor.

• • • • •

Contents

The Heart of the Matter

Keeping Your Faith Clutter-Free

Imagine your employer announces that in two weeks you'll be moving to Vienna, Austria…forever. How would you react? Although you've seen pictures of this beautiful city, you know very little about it. Because of your limited knowledge, you'd probably try to find out everything you can about Vienna before you left. What language is spoken? What's the temperature like? What clothes are most appropriate?

You'd want to obtain or update your passport, secure any other necessary travel documents, and purchase your airline tickets. You'd have to decide what items you want to move with you and which ones to leave behind. You'd arrange to sell your house here and purchase a new one over there. You'd want to exchange your dollars for the proper currency.

But it would be unimaginable to do nothing and simply adopt the "I'll go with the flow" philosophy. Sure, you might be able to rationalize your lack of preparation with thoughts such as:

- "Maybe at the last moment, circumstances will change and I won't have to go."
- "I'll wait until I get there to see what it's really like."
- "I doubt Vienna is any different from where I live now."

Failing to prepare for your journey would be unwise and could result in some disastrous consequences. If you know you're going to make a long trip, you certainly want to be ready for it.

Whether you realize it or not, you will one day take the journey of a lifetime to a foreign land you've never seen. Although your departure time is unknown to you, the hour is already fixed on God's calendar. At a moment known only to Him, you'll leave everything you own and everyone you know, and you'll stand alone before God. He will decide your eternal destiny: heaven or hell. If you wait until that moment to prepare for the journey, you'll have waited too long. The preparations you make in this life will determine how you spend the next one.

Admittedly, this is a sobering thought for anyone, but especially when we're reminded of our mortality. Last year I turned fifty. This milestone event in my life wasn't as bad as I thought it would be. It was worse! Don't misunderstand. I enjoyed all the attention from family, friends, and church members. My congregation held a huge birthday party for me, complete with skits about their aging pastor. Diapers and Metamucil were among the most frequent gifts. It was all great fun.

But after the celebration ended and the humorous cards had been read and discarded, I was left with this stark realization: Without any doubt, I have more years behind me than in front of me. Sometime in the next twenty to thirty years, I'll meet the invisible God about whom I've taught and with whom I've sporadically communicated.

And when that moment arrives, all of my theological speculations will be meaningless. I'll see God as He really is. The only thing that will matter is whether or not my preparation for eternity has been adequate.

Realizing how little time I have left before my inevitable departure has led me to ask myself the simple question, *What does God really want from me?* In my mind, that question has moved from being theoretical to critical. The stakes are too high for me to get it wrong. It's really the only question that matters. In my twenties and thirties, I thought about this question occasionally, but now I awaken in the middle of the night wondering, *What must I do to please God?*

I can already hear some of you shouting back the stock answer: "Robert, you of all people should know that there is nothing you can do to please God. Just trust in Christ as your Savior, and everything will be okay." I've preached that message for years, and I still believe it—to an extent. But let's be honest. When you look at the whole of Scripture, can you honestly say that the only thing God wants from us is a willingness to accept our free ticket to heaven? Again, the stakes are too high for us to be wrong.

At the outset, let me affirm that I definitely believe that salvation from God's eternal judgment comes through faith alone in Jesus Christ. We can do nothing to merit God's forgiveness. "For by grace you have been saved through faith...not as a result of works, that no one should boast" (Ephesians 2:8–9). Those words are more than just an evangelical mantra; they are the bedrock of the Christian faith.

However, an honest search of Scripture reveals that God is interested in more than our justification—our right standing before Him, secured by Christ's death and guaranteeing our entrance into heaven. How do I know that? Consider Jesus's exchange with an attorney who might have been experiencing his own midlife crisis. Perhaps on the morning after his fiftieth birthday, he saw a crowd standing around Jesus and decided to take advantage of the opportunity to speak with the rabbi who was gaining renown throughout Israel.

"Teacher, what shall I do to inherit eternal life?" (Luke 10:25).

Whenever I've taught on this particular passage, I've always claimed that this was an insincere question from someone trying to trap Jesus into contradicting the teaching of the Pharisees. After all, Luke emphasized that the question was meant to "put Him to the test" (verse 25). Maybe the lawyer was fulfilling his assignment from the Pharisees to trick the Lord and destroy His credibility.

Or maybe this lawyer—feeling the signs of his own mortality—thought he might do his assigned job and, at the same time, seek the answer to a question that kept him awake at nights. Regardless of the lawyer's motivation, notice Jesus's answer. He affirms what the lawyer already knows to be true. Interested in eternal life? Then:

> You shall love the LORD your GOD with all your heart, and with
> all your soul, and with all your strength, and will all your mind;
> and your neighbor as yourself. (verse 27)

What's the essence of a right relationship with God? What does our Creator desire from us more than anything else? A heart fully devoted to Him and a heart that loves other people as much as we love ourselves. Simple. Not easy, but simple.

We've all heard our share of fallen-preacher stories, but one that came across my desk recently takes the cake. A prominent church in our denomination had been searching for a pastor for three years. After an exhaustive hunt, the pulpit committee proudly presented the candidate to the church. The first few weeks, the new pastor wowed the congregation with his flamboyant oratorical skills. The crowds began to build almost instantly.

However, a month after arriving at his church, the new pastor submitted a one-paragraph resignation. The reason? A local newspaper had uncovered the truth about this man. His résumé was filled with bogus degrees. Not only that, he'd reportedly embezzled nearly $200,000 from a previous church. And the IRS had been after him as well. When confronted about the negligence in the pulpit committee's research, one member responded, "We were swayed by his unusual ability to communicate the gospel."

Communicate the gospel? What gospel? The gospel that says you can receive your "get out of hell free" card and then live however you choose? The gospel that teaches you can be *forgiven* by Jesus without ever *following* Jesus?

The stunned members of this church were probably left asking, "How could such a thing happen?"

Perhaps Dallas Willard has the answer:

A carefully cultivated heart will, assisted by the grace of God, foresee, forestall, or transform most of the painful situations before which others stand like helpless children saying "Why?"…

Accordingly, the greatest need you and I have—the greatest need of collective humanity—is *renovation of our heart.* That spiritual place within from which outlook, choices, and actions come has been formed by a world away from God. Now it must be transformed.[1]

The essence of the gospel is a changed life that comes from a transformed heart. The apostle Paul wrote, "Therefore if any man is in Christ, he is a new creature; the old things passed away; behold, new things have come" (2 Corinthians 5:17). Unfortunately, too many of us come to the cross of Jesus Christ "just as I am," we receive our pardon from hell, and we leave just as we were. Although the statement has become almost trite, it's still true that no measurable differences exist between the lifestyles of believers and unbelievers. We commit adultery and get divorced at the same rate non-Christians do. We inflate our résumés. We become slaves to various addictions such as prescription drugs and pornography.

I recently received an urgent call from a member of our congregation. His addiction to alcohol and pornography had led to the breakup of his marriage a few hours earlier, and now he was driving himself to a rehabilitation center in another city. He was calling not only to ask for my prayers but to apologize for having to leave his place of service in our church.

"Pastor, it was so exciting to be part of a ministry with a worldwide impact, but my heart was dying on the inside." He went on to compliment the "wonderful teaching" that he said he had heard each week, but frankly his words seemed a little hollow to me.

No matter how orthodox my messages were, they apparently hadn't penetrated his heart. I thought about the plaque one pastor placed on the inside of his pulpit. Every time he stood to preach, he read, "What in the world are you doing to these people?"

I'm asking myself that question a lot these days. What message am I communicating to the people under my spiritual care about their eternal destinies? Is some flaw in my teaching responsible for the lack of measurable change in the lives of my congregants? Is it possible that I've gotten it wrong all these years and have completely missed what God really requires of me? Am I going to be surprised when I stand before God one day and hear His evaluation of my life?

I assume you were attracted to this book because you sincerely want to "get it right" when it comes to your relationship with God. You may or may not have yet crossed the midlife milestone, but something inside you yearns to cut through the clutter of Christianity and discover what God really wants *from* you and *for* you. Face it. Christianity has become unbe-lievably complicated by secondary issues.

One of my recently acquired addictions is reading Christian blogs. A newspaper interviewer asked me recently if I blogged, and I sanctimo-niously responded, "No, I'm too busy trying to share God's Word rather than my musings about life." But my schedule doesn't keep me from *read-ing* the musings of others. Right now some of these blogs are filled with wranglings over theological issues.

Reading these back-and-forth exchanges, you'd think that the ability to precisely parse the correct answers to these issues is what the Christian faith is all about. I like what one person wrote after someone suggested a labo-rious rewording of a particular statement of doctrine: "It seems to me that our personal relationship with Christ should be more enjoyable than doing our taxes."

Again, don't misunderstand. I appreciate the importance of correct the-ology. But do we really think when we get to heaven, God will judge us according to our ability to properly articulate the relationship between His sovereignty and our responsibility? At the judgment seat of Christ, will the Lord distribute blue books to each of us and ask us to diagram the end times?

For the less theologically inclined, the essence of Christianity may be embracing the right cultural causes. After all, they remind us, "Faith with-out works is dead" (James 2:26). Some popular causes we're encouraged to champion include the elimination of poverty in third-world countries; the fight against same-sex marriages; and opposition to abortion, stem-cell research, and human cloning. Again, all worthy causes, to be sure. But as you read the New Testament—written during one of the most morally decadent periods in human history—can you honestly surmise that what God wants most from us is to become cultural warriors?

Are these theological points and cultural matters really the issues about which God is most concerned? Is He waiting breathlessly in heaven and hoping against hope that we're able to formulate a doctrinal statement that explains Him in human terms or to eradicate every social evil on the planet?

The contemporary landscape of Christianity today reminds me of Jesus's admonition to Martha in Luke 10:

> Martha, Martha, you are worried and bothered about so many
> things; but only a few things are necessary, really only one.
> (verses 41–42)

The problem with focusing on secondary concerns is that it causes us to miss what God really desires from us. It's time to cut through the clutter and discover what the Christian faith is really all about.

Clutter-Free Christianity

Hans Hofmann wrote, "The ability to simplify means to eliminate the unnecessary so that the necessary may speak."[2]

The business world increasingly understands the importance of simplicity. Last year both my teenage daughters wanted the same item for Christmas: Apple iPods. After taking out a second mortgage on our home, I was able to purchase these portable musical devices that have sold millions of units. While iPods are expensive, they're also incredibly simple to operate—just one large button in the center with four touch points controls the entire device. Apple successfully reduced complex technology into a simple operating system that anyone can use.

So what can Christians learn from the corporate world? For starters, perhaps the reason our faith seems to make so little difference in our lives is that we've clouded Christianity with secondary concerns and missed the core issue. And maybe we've become so distracted by so many things that we miss the one thing God is most interested in.

The Pharisees had the unusual gift of complicating the simple. They formulated 613 regulations for living. But, as we saw earlier, Jesus reduced these hundreds of laws into two simple principles: love God with all your heart and love others as yourself.

"Wait a minute, Lord! Aren't You forgetting a few things? What about abstaining from immorality, setting aside anger, forgiving those who wrong us, being a good steward of the earth's resources, and the myriad other commands in Scripture? Are You saying You don't care about any of this?"

Of course not. God is concerned about those areas of our lives, and many more. Yet God understands that the basic issue in life is the condition of our heart. Unless our heart is right, nothing else can be right. The writer of Proverbs advised:

Watch over your heart with all diligence,
For from it flow the springs of life. (4:23)

Think about it. Every issue you confront is related to the condition of your heart:

- Whether you continue to be paralyzed by fear over that potential disaster looming on the horizon depends on whether you have a fearful heart or a trusting heart.
- Whether you allow anger to govern your life is determined by whether you have developed a bitter heart or a forgiving heart.
- Whether you allow money to consume your thoughts depends on whether you have a greedy heart or a content heart.

- Whether you ultimately fall into the trap of immorality is
  determined by whether you have an adulterous heart or a
  pure heart.

Christians tend to get it backward when it comes to our relationship with God. We try to modify our behavior without ever doing anything to transform our hearts, where our behavior originates. We join accountability groups to break our addictions. We cut up our charge cards in an attempt to control our spending. And we medicate ourselves to relieve our anxiety. But we still find it impossible to experience victory over pornography, greed, or fear. Why? Because we haven't dealt with the heart of the issue—our heart.

On a Christmas Eve afternoon a few years ago, I was showering, getting ready for our church's annual candlelight service. While I was standing in the stall, a very offensive smell began to suffocate me. Although I'd waited until the afternoon to shower, I quickly realized that I couldn't smell that bad! I looked down and saw the source of the problem. I won't go into the gross details, but all kinds of unspeakable things started gurgling up from the shower drain, over the edge of the shower, and onto the bathroom tile. Merry Christmas!

I quickly leaped out of the shower and yelled for my wife, and we began a serious mop-up operation. Once the floor was clean, I used my vast knowledge of plumbing to fix the problem. Reaching under the bathroom sink, I retrieved a bottle of Drano, poured it down the shower drain, and then turned on the water as the directions dictated. And up—and out—it all came again.

Fortunately, we found a plumber willing to pay a visit on Christmas Eve. He quickly surmised that the problem was not in the drain, but instead could be traced to the sewage line. Some aggressive underground tree roots had clogged the lines and caused the backup of refuse. Only by dealing with the root problem could we be free of the resulting mess.

Every day you and I have offensive thoughts, attitudes, and actions that flow from our hearts. When even *we* are offended by the resulting stench, how must God react?

What can we do about the refuse in our lives? We can spend our time in futile mop-up operations, or we can get to the root of all of our problems: our heart. "Watch over your heart with all diligence." Greed, anger, adultery, addiction, and a thousand other vices aren't our real problem. They're just symptoms of the real problem: a heart that hasn't been properly guarded and cultivated so that it can love God and others fully.

What can we do about the condition of our hearts? More than you might think. Together, we'll discover how we can cooperate with God to transform our hearts—and, as a result, our entire lives.

That's what God really wants from you—and *for* you.

2

Simply Supernatural

Connecting Your Heart to God's Power

Talk about spiritual transformation and you may get glazed looks.

We shouldn't be surprised. Phrases like "conformed to the image of Christ," "obeying Christ in every area of life," or "Christ in you the hope of glory" do little to excite the average Christian. We've heard it all before and have become numb to it.

Yet, in contexts outside of the Bible, the possibility of supernatural transformation seizes our imagination and lies at the heart of our favorite stories.

When I was a child, I dressed up in blue tights and a red cape and sat glued to our black-and-white television set watching *Adventures of Superman.* Millions of children just like me were enthralled by the transformation of mild-mannered reporter Clark Kent into the Man of Steel.

Some fifty years later, the special effects have improved, but the intriguing plot—an ordinary person discovering he has supernatural powers— remains one of our favorite fantasies. Currently, one of the top-rated television programs is about "ordinary people discovering extraordinary abilities." The story involves a genetics professor in India who uncovers the truth that seemingly normal people among us possess supernatural powers. A high school cheerleader learns that she's indestructible, a young dreamer discovers that he can fly, and a down-on-his-luck police officer has the ability to hear what others are thinking.

Why do millions of viewers tune in to this program every week?

Because we're naturally enthralled by the possibility of living a supernatural life.

A True Supernatural Transformation

Being able to reach inside ourselves and access a power that will lift us above our humdrum, everyday existence isn't only intriguing…it really is possible. As a Christian, you've been genetically engineered to transform into someone more super than Superman and more incredible than the Incredible Hulk. You have the extraordinary ability to be transformed into the person of Jesus Christ. Think about that! Within you lies the potential to

- think the thoughts that Jesus thought
- possess the inner peace that Jesus possessed
- enjoy the freedom from material concerns that Jesus enjoyed
- experience the connection to God's power that Jesus experienced
- respond to mistreatment as Jesus responded
- receive the praise from God that Jesus continues to receive

Spiritual transformation is about an ordinary person like you discovering that you indeed have extraordinary abilities…and living accordingly. This is more than the storyline for a television series. It's a reality for everyone who has trusted in Christ as Savior. The apostle Paul described the

Christians in Galatia as "my children, with whom I am again in labor until Christ is *formed* in you" (Galatians 4:19).

This verse is pregnant (pardon the pun) with symbolism. The word *formed* is a translation of the Greek word *morphō,* which describes the growth of an embryo in the mother's womb. Think of the supernatural phenomenon of a tiny fertilized egg morphing into a full-sized and fully functioning human being. That minuscule egg, invisible to the naked eye, possesses all of the energy necessary for transforming itself into a being millions of times larger in size, developing a brain capable of creating a nuclear weapon to destroy the planet where it lives, and interacting in meaningful relationships with other human beings and with its Creator.

Similarly, when you become a Christian, you're impregnated with a "seed…imperishable" (1 Peter 1:23) that contains all of the spiritual energy necessary to morph you into the image of Jesus Christ. In a bit, we'll discuss the way this transformation occurs. But it's that possibility I want you to consider right now.

What God wants *from* you and *for* you—above all else—is for you to resemble Jesus Christ in your attitudes, actions, and affections. In fact, those areas provide a good way to define *spiritual transformation* as meaning "thinking as Jesus thought, doing what Jesus did, and loving what Jesus loved." Consider just some of the many passages in the Bible that describe God's desire for our complete transformation:

> For whom He foreknew, He also predestined to become *conformed* to the image of His Son, that He might be the first-born among many brethren. (Romans 8:29)

> And do not be conformed to this world, but be *transformed* by the renewing of your mind. (Romans 12:2)

But we all…are being *transformed* into the same image from glory to glory, just as from the Lord, the Spirit. (2 Corinthians 3:18)

Christ in you, the hope of glory. (Colossians 1:27)

I'll confess to you that the above words didn't excite me that much—not initially. I've read these verses and heard so many sermons using the phrase "conformed to the image of Christ" that I almost put myself to sleep when I preach the same message to my congregation or write this message to you. Why is that?

Familiarity breeds contempt…and boredom. Anything you hear repeatedly—especially if it involves the same words—can anesthetize your response. But I believe the primary cause of the apathetic feeling most of us have about spiritual transformation (go ahead, you can admit it) is our failure to grasp the benefits of such a life. We'll discuss this more in the next section, but you'll never be excited about something—much less pursue something—until you believe it will benefit you.

Consider for a moment some benefits that you'd enjoy if you could miraculously morph into Jesus Christ. Imagine a life where:

- You were completely free from worry about *anything*.
- You felt content about your financial situation.
- You had no ill feelings toward anyone.
- You weren't enslaved to any destructive habits.
- Your outward circumstances had no effect on your inward happiness.
- You had the assurance that God was pleased with your life.

This kind of life isn't a pipe dream. It's a possibility. How do I know? Because this is exactly the kind of life that Jesus lived, and the embryo of His life has been implanted in each of us who knows Him. What we must do to ensure the growth of that embryo into the full-grown person of Christ in us is the subject matter of this book.

However, to clearly understand what spiritual transformation is, we need to clarify what it isn't. I grew up in a family that didn't have much money but loved ice cream. Sometimes when we found ourselves running out of money before we ran out of month, my parents would purchase a substitute ice cream called mellorine for forty-nine cents a gallon. Only aging Baby Boomers might remember the name—or the awful taste—of this poor man's ice cream. But trust me, a few servings of mellorine could quench your desire for any kind of frozen dessert, including ice cream.

Author John Ortberg identifies two cheap substitutes for spiritual transformation that, like mellorine, squelch our desire for the real thing; in place of being transformed, some Christians settle for being informed or conformed. I define these cheap substitutes as follows:

Informed

It's far too easy to equate spiritual information with spiritual transformation. For some believers, the goal of the Christian life involves learning as much about the Bible and theology as possible. They think this knowledge will somehow magically and automatically transform them into the kind of people they should be. If that's true, why are knowledgeable Christians some of the meanest people on earth? Why do gifted teachers of the Word regularly fall into sexual immorality and addictions? Why do we hear so many stories of well-taught believers completely abandoning their beliefs?

Conformed

For other Christians, conforming to some man-made system of beliefs and behavior is equated with spiritual transformation. According to Ortberg, many religious groups establish "boundary markers"—highly visible and usually superficial standards of dress, behavior, or beliefs that help the group distinguish who is in the club and who is outside the club. Unfortunately, many Christians in these subsets (commonly known as denominations) confuse conformation to these artificial standards with spiritual transformation.

For the purpose of full disclosure, I'm part of a religious denomination known for such artificial boundaries. If asked to define a Southern Baptist, the average person off the street would probably say, "Someone who doesn't drink, dance, or have any fun." Some of my Baptist brethren are probably insulted by that caricature, protesting that no such standard is embraced today. Maybe that's true, but we Baptists are constantly tempted to adopt some new artificial standards to help us maintain our identity. Last year a leader in our denomination said that we needed to take a stand against contemporary praise music. When asked why, he responded, "How else can we distinguish ourselves as Baptists?" Although he was resoundingly criticized by fellow leaders, his attitude reflects that of many Christians who have confused conformation to a man-made standard with spiritual transformation.

In Jesus's day, the Pharisees adopted conformation as their preferred substitute for spiritual transformation. They established a superficial standard of conduct, prided themselves for adherence to it, and criticized anyone who didn't conform. Jesus, in turn, criticized *them* for missing the whole point:

> Woe to you, scribes and Pharisees, hypocrites! For you clean the
> outside of the cup and of the dish, but inside they are full of rob-
> bery and self-indulgence. You blind Pharisee, first clean the inside of
> the cup and of the dish, so that the outside of it may become clean
> also. (Matthew 23:25–26)

What God really desires from you isn't a head filled with information, and God also isn't interested in your conformation to some superficial standard of behavior. What God wants for you is a complete transformation of your entire life.

If He has already planted the possibility for such a change within you, what hinders that transformation in your life? I believe Christians fail to experience spiritual transformation for the following misguided reasons.

It's Not Necessary

Perhaps the most pervasive reason Christians fail to become the kind of people God wants them to be is the mistaken idea that spiritual transformation is nice, but not necessary. Receiving my free ticket to heaven is what really matters; anything beyond that is optional. Allowing God to reign over my thoughts, actions, and attitudes is like an upgrade from coach to first-class—a luxury reserved only for those who care to pay the extra price.

But is that really the message of the New Testament? Did Jesus make allowance for belief without obedience? Read what Scripture says about Jesus and then decide for yourself:

> He who believes in the Son has eternal life; but he who does not
> obey the Son shall not see life, but the wrath of God abides on
> him. (John 3:36)

> If anyone serves Me, let him follow Me. (John 12:26)

> He who has My commandments and keeps them, he it is who
> loves Me; and he who loves Me shall be loved by My Father, and
> I will love him, and will disclose Myself to him. (John 14:21)

He who does not love Me does not keep My words. (John 14:24)

I like the old joke about a man who died after living a godless, immoral life. To his surprise, however, he found himself in a world of bright sunlight, soft music, and people all dressed in white.

I sure never expected to wind up here, he thought to himself. *I suppose God must have a soft spot in His heart for people like me.* He turned to one of the figures dressed in white and said, "Can I buy you a drink? I've got something to celebrate."

"If you are referring to an alcoholic beverage, we don't serve those here," the angel responded.

"No booze, huh? Well, how about a game of poker?"

"Sir, we don't gamble here, either," the angelic figure replied.

The man was perplexed. "Then what do you do around here all day?"

"Well, we sing a lot of hymns. There is a Bible study every morning and a prayer meeting every afternoon."

"Hymns, prayer meetings, Bible studies? Boy, heaven is not what it's cracked up to be."

The figure in white smiled. "You don't understand. We're in heaven; you're in hell."

Behind this cute story is the profound truth that heaven is reserved for those who love praising God, talking to God, and obeying God. It's illogical to think that we could spend our entire lives rebelling against God's rule over our life on earth and then want to spend eternity submitting to His authority in heaven. Dallas Willard wrote:

One should seriously inquire if to live in a world permeated with God and the knowledge of God is something they themselves truly desire. If not, they can be assured that God will excuse them from his presence. They will find their place in the "outer darkness" of which Jesus spoke. But the fundamental fact about them will not be that they are there, but that they have become people so locked into their own self-worship and denial of God that *they cannot want God*.[1]

It's Not Desirable

Have you noticed that we often consider the unpleasant things of life as being optional? Exercise, diets, and controlling our spending aren't practiced behaviors because they aren't desired behaviors. For the most part, we end up doing the things that we really want to do. Taking a vacation with my family each summer, watching the next episode of *24* each week, and eating a bowl of Häagen Dazs vanilla ice cream each night might not always be possible, yet I'll try to find a way to do these things simply because I want to do them.

The same principle is at work in our relationship with God. I appreciate the honesty of this simple prayer: "Lord, I don't love You. I don't even want to love You. But I want to want to love You." Perhaps you've felt the same way about the subject of spiritual transformation: "Lord, I'm not like Jesus. I don't even want to be like Jesus. But I want to want to be like Jesus." We must want to want to be like Jesus before we'll ever become like Jesus. And that means being convinced that spiritual transformation is really something desirable.

To be like Jesus means to live like Jesus, and that means allowing God to have the final say in every part of life. The essence of spiritual transformation—the essence of living in the kingdom of God—is submitting to God's rule in all aspects of our lives. The central message of Jesus Christ concerned the kingdom of God:

Jesus was going about in all Galilee, teaching in their synagogues, and proclaiming the gospel of the kingdom. (Matthew 4:23)

As you go, preach, saying, "The kingdom of heaven is at hand." (Matthew 10:7)

He said to them, "I must preach the kingdom of God to the other cities also, for I was sent for this purpose." (Luke 4:43)

What is the "kingdom of God" or the "kingdom of heaven" that Jesus announced and invites us to participate in? It's actually quite simple. A monarch's kingdom consists of the territory he rules. Within that piece of real estate, whatever the king wants done, the king gets done.

While it's true that God is sovereign (a word simply meaning "in charge") over all creation, He has chosen to allow a rebellion against His will in one small portion of the universe. That territory is the human heart. But the condition is only temporary.

One day God's authority will be recognized and obeyed by everyone on the planet. Some refer to that period of time as "the Millennium" (the thousand-year rule of Christ on the earth) while others call it the "new heaven and the new earth" described in Revelation 21. Regardless of what you name it, Old Testament prophets like Isaiah eagerly anticipated this time when all the earth would submit to God's rule:

But with righteousness He will judge the poor,
    And decide with fairness for the afflicted of the earth....
And the wolf will dwell with the lamb,
    And the leopard will lie down with the kid....

They will not hurt or destroy in all My holy mountain,
    For the earth will be full of the knowledge of the LORD
    As the waters cover the sea. (Isaiah 11:4, 6, 9)

Can you imagine how magnificent it will be to live in a world where whatever God wants done, gets done? The poor are no longer taken advantage of. The afflicted are relieved of their problems. No one mistreats another person. Everyone submits to God's will.

Relegating this kingdom of God exclusively to some future period in history, however, unnecessarily postpones the benefits of living under God's perfect and protective reign. In a sense, we can experience the kingdom of God right now. How?

Jesus told a series of stories in Matthew 13 to illustrate how God's kingdom secretly operates in the hearts of individuals who submit themselves to His authority. While God's rule over the entire earth has been postponed until Christ's return to earth, we can still experience the benefits of God's rule in our personal lives. And those benefits have incomparable value, as Jesus illustrated in this brief parable:

> The kingdom of heaven is like a treasure hidden in the field, which
> a man found and hid; and from joy over it he goes and sells all that
> he has, and buys that field. (verse 44)

Some years ago our family owned some farmland that we sold for what we thought was a fair price. Little did we know that underneath that land was one of the largest reserves of natural gas in this part of the country. Had we retained the mineral rights, I'd probably be enjoying life on a tropical island somewhere.

Interestingly, last week an attorney called me and said he believed there was a chance that we'd retained a minuscule claim on the rights to that land. Since that time, I've had visions of Jed Clampett dancing in my head! We're willing to go to extensive trouble and expense to prove our small interest in that property because of its great value.

The man in Jesus's parable had a similar experience. The treasure he discovered in a field he didn't own was so valuable that he was willing to pay any price to obtain title to that land.

Jesus was teaching that if we really understand the value of the kingdom of God, we'll be willing to pay any price and expend every effort necessary to obtain it.

Instead of limiting the kingdom of God to heaven or to some future period in time, we need to understand that the kingdom of God is anyplace where God's will is being obeyed. Isn't that what Jesus taught in the model prayer?

Thy kingdom come,
Thy will be done,
On earth as it is in heaven. (Matthew 6:10)

Right now God's will is being accomplished in heaven. We should pray for the time when God's will shall be done on earth. And in the meantime we can experience the incomparable benefits of God's will being accomplished in our own lives.

First, however, we must be persuaded that submission to God's will is really desirable…and we aren't fully convinced of that, are we? In fact, we believe the opposite. We've allowed the Enemy to deceive us into believing that God's rule over our:

- sexual lives will result in frustration
- vocations will result in our living in a hut in Africa
- dreams will result in disappointment
- desire for significance will result in obscurity
- finances will result in poverty
- relationships will result in loneliness

Don't believe any of that for a moment. Satan is "a liar and the father of lies," Jesus said (John 8:44, NIV). The truth is that submitting to God's authority in our lives results in:

- freedom from worry
- contentment with our finances
- harmony in our relationships
- power over destructive addictions
- inner peace in spite of outward circumstances

Jesus experienced all of this and more because He placed every part of His life under God's rule. His experience can be your experience if you're willing to make the effort to allow Christ's life to be formed in you.

It's Not Possible

Another misconception that keeps us from experiencing spiritual transformation is that we don't think it can happen. I might, for example, wish I were six feet tall. I wish I'd win the lottery. I'd like to speak several languages fluently. I'd like to win the Pulitzer Prize. All of those objectives are desirable, but they're either not possible or not probable. So why try?

After reading about the invaluable benefits of living under God's complete rule of your life, you might have sensed your spirit starting to soar a little as you began to imagine what such an existence would be like. Then reality set in as you realized that every resolution you've ever made to change has resulted in disappointment:

- You've never had any power over your appetites.
- Worrying seems to be your favorite pastime.
- You find it impossible to forgive those who have hurt you deeply.
- You feel that you're slipping further and further away from God.

So why attempt to do something you know is impossible? Why add to your list of broken resolutions? Living like Jesus Christ may be desirable, but we've convinced ourselves that it's beyond our reach.

Recently I saw a cartoon on the editorial page of a national newspaper. The first frame pictured a television reporter announcing, "The government is now targeting single adults with its abstinence-only program." In the second frame the reporter continued, "Future programs will try to keep birds from flying and fish from swimming."

Such cynicism about our ability to overcome our natural impulses has crept into the Christian world as well. Say no to sex outside of marriage? Resist the impulse to hurt those who hurt us? Separate our inward peace from our outward circumstances? Refuse to worry about the future? Experience contentment regardless of our income? As the *Seinfeld* character Kramer would say, "That's kooky talk!" It's just not natural.

That's right. It's *supernatural,* meaning it's above the natural. But supernatural living is possible because of the supernatural power every Christian possesses. Paul explained:

For the power of the life-giving Spirit—and this power is mine
through Christ Jesus—has freed me from the vicious circle of sin
and death…. So now we can obey God's laws if we follow after

the Holy Spirit and no longer obey the old evil nature within us.
(Romans 8:2, 4, TLB)

It's Not Planned For

Finally, we don't experience spiritual transformation because we don't plan for it. Imagine that, after fifteen years of living in your present home, you decide to make a change. The demands of a growing family coupled with the natural deterioration of your current residence require you to do something. However, the memories you've built in your current home and your enjoyment of the neighborhood cause you to rule out both moving to another house and completely leveling the one you occupy. What you really want isn't a completely new home, but a renovated home.

You can envision the benefits of expanded living areas, fresh paint, and updated appliances. Yes, an extensive renovation will be costly and messy, but the finished product will be well worth the effort. Maybe an unexpected inheritance from a dear old aunt means you can afford the project.

However, determining that the renovation is necessary, desirable, and possible isn't enough. You need to create a plan to execute and complete the project. You need to take such steps as selecting an architect to design the plans for the renovation, establishing a budget, setting a schedule, and hiring a contractor. And, of course, laborers must actually do the work. Renovations don't happen automatically.

Could it be that one reason you and I aren't experiencing the kind of spiritual transformation I've described so far is that we don't have a plan for the renovation of our attitudes, actions, and affections? Think about it. What plan do you have for any of the following?

- freeing yourself from concerns about money
- conquering those addictions that are destroying your life

- refusing to allow resentment to be your response to mistreatment
- making obedience to God's commands your normal response

This kind of spiritual transformation doesn't just happen. Again, believing that such transformation is essential, desirable, and possible isn't enough. We must develop a plan—and execute it.

Costly? You better believe it.

Difficult? Without a doubt.

But the finished product is well worth the effort.

Heart Surgery

Experiencing Heaven on Earth Now

If I asked you, "Do you desire to be part of the kingdom of God?" you would probably answer, "Of course!" No one wants to be excluded from God's kingdom. After all, Jesus described life outside of God's kingdom as a place of "outer darkness" where "weeping and gnashing of teeth" take place (Matthew 22:13).

Who wants to end up there?

Yet when we refuse to submit our will to God's will, we are making a conscious choice to live outside God's kingdom. The kingdom of God isn't just a synonym for heaven. Yes, heaven—and the new earth—will be the ultimate expression of God's kingdom, because everyone who inhabits them will submit to God's rule. Likewise, hell will be the ultimate expression of life outside the kingdom of God, because hell's occupants will be those who have continually rebelled against God's rule.

But that clear delineation between those living inside and those living outside God's kingdom exists right now. An analogy will help make this point. A monarch's kingdom describes the realm where his commands are revered and obeyed. For example, the queen of England is sovereign over British territory, but she has absolutely no authority over me since I don't live in an area within the kingdom of Great Britain. I live outside her kingdom. In the same way, people who live in God's kingdom recognize, respect, and submit to God's authority. Those living outside the kingdom don't recognize God's rule over their lives. Heaven and hell are, therefore, the eternal continuation of our present choice.

Just as we will enjoy the future, eternal benefits of living within the kingdom of God (think: bodies that never age, the absence of sickness and sadness, reunion with loved ones) rather than living outside the kingdom of God (think: infinite darkness, intense loneliness, eternal pain), we can also experience the present benefits of living under God's rule. In the previous chapter I tried to paint a picture of what a life under God's rule looked like. We tend, however, to take a detour that leads us away from experiencing His kingdom. Allow me to illustrate by going back to the kingdom of Great Britain.

By sipping tea every afternoon, changing my accent, wearing only Turnbull and Asser ties, and learning the words to the British national anthem, I can resemble a British citizen without ever becoming one. However, becoming a British citizen and living as a British citizen involve more than simply mimicking the behavior of a British citizen.

Similarly, focusing on changing our external behavior in order to resemble a citizen of God's kingdom isn't enough. Being content with our financial situation, forgiving others, giving up worrying, and trusting God more are all good things to do. But without experiencing an inward transformation that makes those behaviors both desirable and habitual, they're impossible to do. Until we realize that, we'll sentence ourselves to a lifetime of mopping up the messes (remember my shower story?) that emanate from a heart that hasn't been transformed.

In this chapter, I want us to consider where spiritual transformation takes place, who is responsible for the transformation, and the way it occurs.

The Heart of the Matter

A short course in biblical anatomy can help us understand the way we can become the kind of people God desires. Before we can grasp how we can be transformed, though, we need to understand *what* needs to be transformed.

We've been heavily influenced by Greek philosophy, which separates the mind from the heart. We think of the mind as the center of our thoughts, our decisions, and even the awareness of our existence ("I think, therefore I am"). And we view the heart as the center of our emotions—love, hate, happiness, sadness.

However, the writers of Scripture saw the heart as the center of our being that governs all aspects of our lives. For example, the heart is pictured as the center of our intellect: "For as he thinks within himself, so he is" (Proverbs 23:7). Jesus addressed the scribes who questioned His deity by asking, "Why are you reasoning about these things *in your hearts*?" (Mark 2:8).

Our will to take or not take certain actions also originates within our hearts. The Pharisees decided in their hearts to reject Christ: "And after looking around at them with anger, grieved at their hardness of *heart*..." (Mark 3:5).

Although the Bible occasionally identifies the bowels as the center of our emotions, at other times the heart determines whether we experience joy, sadness, anxiety, or peace. The two people who encountered Christ on the road to Emmaus after His resurrection said, "Were not our *hearts* burning within us while He was speaking to us on the road...?" (Luke 24:32).

Your thoughts, your will, and your emotions are the essential components of who you are. Since these all come from the heart, the simplest way to define the heart is to say that your heart represents *you;* your heart is the sum total of who you are. That explains why God declared, "Man looks at the outward appearance, but the LORD looks at the heart" (1 Samuel 16:7).

The anger you feel when a driver cuts you off, the exhilaration you feel during a powerful worship service, the anguish you experience when a friend dies, or the magnetic attraction that draws you toward your mate all originate in your heart.

The apostle Paul recognized the difference between the *visible* you and the *real* you. The visible you is your body, which begins slowly deteriorating the moment you're born and seems to reach warp speed after age fifty (do I hear an "Amen"?). But we can find a silver lining in that dark reality:

> Therefore we do not lose heart, but though our outer man is decaying,
> yet our inner man is being renewed day by day. (2 Corinthians 4:16)

While the visible you is decaying, the real you (known as "the inner man" or "the heart") can be transformed. When we speak of the transformation of the heart, we're talking about the transformation of our thoughts, our emotions, and our will. In other words, a spiritual transformation is a complete overhaul of your heart, a complete overhaul of who you really are. Why is such an extensive renovation necessary? I can think of at least two reasons.

Thoughts, Will, and Feelings Determine Behavior

Acts of sexual immorality, financial dishonesty, violence, or deception aren't involuntary responses. Instead, they are the natural by-product or fruit of the kind of heart we have. As Jesus said,

The good man out of his good treasure brings forth what is good;
and the evil man out of his evil treasure brings forth what is evil.
(Matthew 12:35)

To attempt to change our behavior without changing the condition of our hearts is an exercise in futility. For example, how many diets have you started...and quit? How many New Year's resolutions have you kept past January? How many times have you promised God, "Never again will I..." only to find yourself engaging in the same behavior before the end of the week—or day?

Let me offer an example. And I know I risk offending some people by stating this, but we set up teenagers for failure when we encourage them to make pledges of sexual abstinence, place rings on their fingers, and invite them to enter into a covenant with God without dealing with the deeper issues of the heart.

In fact, more harm than good may come from such attempts at behavior modification without a heart renovation. Imagine that a teenager attends a weekend seminar where she hears about God's plan for sex and marriage as well as the emotional and physical risks of promiscuity. The speaker challenges her to make a decision to abstain from sex until marriage. In an emotion-packed closing session, she signs a pledge indicating her intention to remain sexually pure until marriage.

However, the following Friday night, in a moment of heated passion, she breaks that pledge. Her profound disappointment in herself not only results in understandable guilt over her broken pledge, but it also leads her to the conclusion that she's incapable of controlling or changing her behavior. Her well-intentioned youth leaders have actually performed a great disservice.

By failing to understand and therefore address the inadequacy of decisions or "resolves" alone to control and change behavior, youth pastors have convinced her that such control and change are impossible. In fact, they have unwittingly assured that she'll probably be more promiscuous than before the weekend seminar because she now has evidence that purity is impossible.

Any attempt to instigate, eliminate, or modify behavior that doesn't deal with a transformation of our heart—of our thoughts, our affections, and our will—*will* fail.

Pollution of the Heart

The Bible contains several descriptions of our heart in its natural state—and none of them is pretty. In Genesis 6:5, God offers this analysis of the condition of the human heart:

> Then the LORD saw that the wickedness of man was great on the
> earth, and that every intent of the thoughts of his heart was only
> evil continually.

Through Jeremiah the prophet, God said this:

> The heart is more deceitful than all else
> And is desperately sick;
> Who can understand it? (17:9)

The Bible traces our heart disease back to Adam and Eve's initial rebellion against God:

> Therefore, just as through one man sin entered into the world, and
> death through sin, and so death spread to all men, because all
> sinned. (Romans 5:12)

You and I have inherited diseased, defective hearts. Probably the best term to describe the condition of our heart—and, as a result, the condition of us—is "ungodly." Scripture uses the term *ungodly* as a designation not just for the dregs of humanity such as child abusers, murderers, and drug addicts, but also as a general classification of the entire human race:

> For while we were still helpless, at the right time Christ died for the ungodly. (Romans 5:6)

Christ's death wasn't reserved for the worst of humanity, but for all of humanity—"the ungodly"—and that includes you and me. In our language, we use the prefix *un-* to mean "not." Someone who is *un*friendly is not friendly. Someone who is *un*attractive is not attractive. So we assume that to be *un*godly is to be not like God.

But the Greek prefix translated "un-" doesn't mean we're simply not like God. It means we are against God. To be ungodly means to be against God in our thoughts, our will, and our emotions—and that's the natural condition of our heart. We're predisposed to oppose God. When God says, "You shall," we instinctively respond, "I shall not." When God says, "You shall not," we automatically reply, "You wanna bet?"

Of course this is an unpopular diagnosis of the human condition. But all you have to do is look around you—and within you—to realize it's an accurate one.

The good news is that, although our hearts are naturally defective, they can be changed. The Old Testament anticipated the time when God would perform heart transplants in His followers:

> And I shall give them one heart, and shall put a new spirit within them. And I shall take the heart of stone out of their flesh and give

them a heart of flesh, that they may walk in My statutes and keep
My ordinances, and do them. (Ezekiel 11:19–20)

Notice the sequence here. Above all things, God desires our obedience—walking in His statutes and keeping His ordinances. But that radical change in our behavior will never occur unless we have a new heart. This leads to a logical question: whose responsibility is it to perform this operation?

The above passage indicates that God is the One who gives His followers a new heart. Yet all we have to do is look around and look within to quickly realize that transformations of the heart are neither automatic nor even common for most Christians.

Let's look more closely at God's responsibility and our responsibility in this entire process of spiritual transformation.

Spiritual Transformation: Who Does It?

Perhaps you've had the experience of attending a meeting where, after much deliberation and brainstorming, the group agrees on a certain course of action to achieve its goal. Yet several weeks later, when the group reconvenes, absolutely no progress has been made toward the objective. Why? Not because the goal wasn't worthy, and not because of a secret plan to subvert the goal. Instead, nothing happened because there wasn't a clear delegation of responsibility. People left the first meeting assuming someone else was responsible for the execution of the plan.

After years of leading a staff, I've discovered—the hard way—that no plan is complete until everyone clearly understands the specific action steps necessary to accomplish the goal and a clear division of responsibility has been established. Specific plans like that ensure that the goal becomes reality. It's far too easy to end a meeting prematurely, especially after experiencing the euphoria of consensus, and not do the grunt work of nailing down the details of who is responsible for what.

This principle also applies to the hard work of spiritual transformation. You may agree that having the real you—that is, your heart—become like Jesus Christ is a desirable goal. You might even be excited about the possibility of experiencing right now the benefits of living in the kingdom of God rather than postponing those benefits until you die.

But a year from now, you'll be exactly the same person you are today unless you have a clearly defined plan for spiritual transformation. Of course, central to that plan is understanding *who* is responsible for the radical change God wants you to experience.

God's Power, Our Effort

A lie has permeated much of today's teaching about Christian living. This lie has been so prevalent for so long that most believers automatically accept it as fact. This lie seems logical and even biblical—and this lie is absolutely lethal to your spiritual transformation. Here it is: "You don't have to exert any effort to become like Jesus Christ. God alone is responsible for your spiritual transformation. Anything you do is operating 'in the flesh.'"

Have you heard that one before? Proponents of this myth even cite Scripture to justify their belief. A favorite passage is Galatians 3:3:

Are you so foolish? Having begun by the Spirit, are you now being perfected by the flesh?

The popular but wrong interpretation of the above verse is "just as you were saved without any effort on your part, you're also transformed into the person God wants you to be without any work." But this interpretation completely ignores the context of the verse. Paul wasn't addressing the topic of sanctification (the theological term that describes spiritual transformation—which is indeed a work of God). Instead, Paul was writing about justification (the theological term describing our legal standing before God once we trust in Christ for salvation).

Paul was simply saying that it makes no sense to try to mix grace and works. To initially receive God's forgiveness by faith in God's grace and then revert to a system of good works to earn God's approval is like mixing oil and water.

Although grace and effort are antithetical to one another when it comes to our justification, both are necessary when it comes to our sanctification. In *Your God Is Too Safe,* Mark Buchanan wrote this:

> Grace and effort are not opposites. Grace and *earning* are opposites. *Working for* your salvation is heresy. *Working out* your salvation is basic Bible. Grace and effort are allies.[1]

Consider just a sampling of Paul's writings where he emphasized the place of working, striving, or exerting effort in our spiritual lives:

> Only conduct yourselves in a manner worthy of the gospel of Christ; so that whether I come and see you or remain absent, I may hear of you that you are standing firm in one spirit, with one mind striving together for the faith of the gospel. (Philippians 1:27)

> So then, my beloved, just as you have always obeyed, not as in my presence only, but now much more in my absence, work

out your salvation with fear and trembling; for it is God who is
at work in you, both to will and to work for His good pleasure.
(2:12–13)

And we proclaim Him, admonishing every man and teaching every
man with all wisdom, that we may present every man complete in
Christ. And for this purpose also I labor, striving according to His
power, which mightily works within me. (Colossians 1:28–29)

Don't misunderstand what I'm saying. God's power is indispensable
to our becoming like Jesus Christ. However, God's power isn't enough to
change us. Yes, you read that correctly. As heretical as that statement sounds,
it's true. God's plan for your spiritual transformation is a partnership
between you and Him. He agrees to supply the power, but He asks you to
supply the effort. Consider once again Paul's command to the Philippian
Christians:

Work out your salvation with fear and trembling; for it is God who
is at work in you, both to will and to work for His good pleasure.
(Philippians 2:12–13)

Salvation involves more than the assurance that one day we'll be in
heaven. In its fullest sense, salvation is our complete deliverance from pat-
terns of thoughts and behaviors that prevent us from experiencing the
kingdom of God right now. Paul never said to work *for* our salvation, but
he did command us to work *out* our salvation, knowing that while we're
working it out, God is working within us, supplying us with all the supernatural power we need to overhaul our thoughts, will, and emotions.

The moment you trust in Christ as your Savior, God equips you with a power (a Person known as the Holy Spirit) containing everything you need to experience a complete spiritual transformation:

> Seeing that His divine power has granted to us everything pertaining to life and godliness...that...you might become partakers of the divine nature. (2 Peter 1:3–4)

Think of it! God has already given you everything you need to live the kind of supernatural life that Jesus Christ lived. But possessing those spiritual resources doesn't automatically ensure spiritual transformation. God supplies the power, but you must supply the effort:

> Now for this very reason also, applying all diligence, *in your faith*
> supply moral excellence, and in your moral excellence, knowledge;
> and in your knowledge, self-control, and in your self-control,
> perseverance, and in your perseverance, godliness; and in your
> godliness, brotherly kindness, and in your brotherly kindness,
> Christian love. (verses 5–7)

Picture an electrical outlet in your home. Behind that outlet is the energy you need to accomplish all kinds of tasks: you can power an oven to cook a fabulous meal, power a sweeper to clean a dirty carpet, power a saw to create a piece of furniture, or power a computer to write a book. But power alone isn't enough to complete any of those tasks. They all require effort on your part.

Similarly, spiritual transformation is a joint project involving God's power and our effort. Without God's power, we *can't* become like Christ. Without our effort, we *won't* become like Christ.

Spiritual Transformation: The Process

Spiritual transformation in our lives doesn't just happen. It's a process involving both God's power and our efforts. Specifically, that process involves three key components: desire, a detailed plan, and discipline. Let's look at each of these.

Desire

We'll never become like Jesus Christ in our actions, attitudes, and affections until we desire to become like Jesus. I remember an old song we used to sing in church when I was a boy. It was a simple hymn that we'd sing to prepare us for a coming revival: "Lord, I want to be a Christian, in my heart, in my heart... Lord, I want to be like Jesus, in my heart, in my heart." That simple song teaches a profound truth: without a heartfelt desire to change, we'll never experience transformation. Any significant change in our life comes from the heart.

Even from the start of our relationship with God, the decision to become a Christian comes from the heart. Paul promised

> That if you confess with your mouth Jesus as Lord, and believe in
> your heart that God raised Him from the dead, you shall be saved.
> (Romans 10:9)

Our continued obedience to the commands of Christ also comes from the heart. Paul wrote to the Ephesians about "doing the will of God from the heart" (6:6).

Yet apart from a supernatural act of God, we'll never have the desire to become a Christian or to live as a Christian. Why? Simply put, our hearts are spiritually dead. Paul described our condition this way:

And you were dead in your trespasses and sins, in which you formerly walked according to the course of this world, according to the prince of the power of the air, of the spirit that is now working in the sons of disobedience. Among them we too all formerly lived in the lusts of our flesh, indulging the desires of the flesh and of the mind, and were by nature children of wrath, even as the rest. (Ephesians 2:1–3)

Have you ever seen a corpse? As a pastor, I see dead people regularly. I've watched family members and friends walk by an open casket and say about the dearly departed, "Doesn't he look good!" Good? I don't think so. No amount of work by the mortician can ever make a corpse look good. It looks dead! Although the corpse may have all the essential body parts—head, hands, feet, lungs, and even a heart—it's completely unaware of anything or anyone around it.

Similarly, while non-Christians might appear to be alive, they are, in fact, spiritually dead. They walk, they talk, they laugh, they cry, but they are completely numb to the spiritual realm of life. They can't respond to the true God because they have no awareness of God or any desire to obey Him. They are completely controlled by "the lusts of [their] flesh."

So how does a spiritually dead person become spiritually alive? Only by the grace and power of God.

But God, being rich in mercy, because of His great love with which He loved us, even when we were dead in our transgressions, made us alive together with Christ (by grace you have been saved). (verses 4–5)

Recently I was watching a television program where the main character's heart stopped beating, and it looked as if his life was over. But then a doctor yelled, "Get the paddles." The nurses ripped open the star's shirt, applied two electrical paddles to his chest, and then sent a surge of electricity through his body that restarted his heart, bringing him back from death—and ensuring another episode of the show!

That's a picture of what God does for us when He saves us. Through the power of the Holy Spirit, God takes a spiritually dead heart and reenergizes it. Once our spiritual heart begins beating, our spiritual eyes are opened, and we become aware of the presence of God. We call upon Him to save us from our sins. We have a new desire to please Him in every aspect of our lives. He equips us with a permanent power source—the Holy Spirit—who supplies us with both the continuing desire and the ability to become like Christ.

A Detailed Plan

The desire and the power to follow through on that desire aren't enough for spiritual transformation. We also need a strategy.

Recently I experienced my own kind of awakening. For a few weeks I had noticed that my pants were getting increasingly tight around the waist. I felt slightly sluggish. I didn't want to accept what I thought was happening, but when I stepped on the scales, my fears were confirmed. I'd gained about seven pounds.

I possess both the desire and the ability to shed that unwanted weight. But desire and ability aren't enough to accomplish the task. I have to establish a plan: I'll increase the time I exercise by 10 percent, I'll cut down on the amount of ice cream I consume, I'll cut out the butter I pour on my popcorn, and so on.

If my physical transformation requires a plan, why should I be surprised that my spiritual transformation needs one too? It's not enough to desire to become like Jesus. Wanting to be more forgiving, less greedy, more trusting, and less fearful are all worthy goals. But we have to have a plan—and that's what this book is all about.

Discipline

I can want to lose weight and even establish a plan to lose weight, but then comes the hard part. What about those mornings I'd rather pull the covers over my head than climb out of bed and onto the treadmill? And how will I react when a particularly tough day at the office causes me to crave some comfort food? Desire and detailed planning aren't enough to achieve a desired goal. Success also takes discipline. I've heard a lot of definitions of *discipline* through the years, and for me this is the best one:

> Discipline is doing what you know you should do
> when you don't feel like doing it.

Nothing worthwhile in life happens without discipline. The late baseball great Ted Williams was known as a "natural hitter." Yet when he was asked about this "natural" ability, Williams replied, "There is no such thing as a natural born hitter. I became a good hitter because I paid the price of constant practice, constant practice." Ted Williams had a desire to be a great hitter. He established a plan of practice that would sharpen his skill. And, ultimately, he had to be willing to be disciplined—to say no to what he wanted to do in order to do what he should do—in order to move from mediocrity to excellence.

Even though God's power has jolted you into spiritual life and infused you with a desire to live like Christ, you still have the powerful headwind of habits to overcome. Before we become Christians, getting even with those who mistreat us, becoming preoccupied with money, indulging our sexual desires, and putting our needs above the needs of other people might be a way of life.

When we commit our lives to Christ, we might realize that these behaviors are wrong. We might truly desire to live differently, yet we've become prisoners of our habits. To truly break free and live differently will require discipline. Elton Trueblood has written this:

> Acceptance of discipline is the price of freedom. The pole vaulter is not free to go over the high bar except as he disciplines himself rigorously day after day. The freedom of the surgeon to use his drill to cut away the bony structure, close to a tiny nerve without severing it, arises from a similar discipline. It is doubtful if excellence in any field comes in any other way.[2]

Paul understood the importance of discipline in spiritual transformation, which is why he encouraged Timothy with these words:

> Discipline yourself for the purpose of godliness; for bodily discipline is only of little profit, but godliness is profitable for all things, since it holds promise for the present life and also for the life to come. (1 Timothy 4:7–8)

The word *discipline* is a translation of the Greek word *gumnos* from which we derive our word *gymnasium*. When I picture a gymnasium, I think about that unmistakable aroma present in every gym I've ever been in. That smell is the natural by-product of bodily perspiration—a.k.a. sweat—that comes from physical exertion.

Becoming godly requires its own measure of holy sweat. It might mean getting up earlier, staying up later, spending thirty minutes on your knees in prayer or in the Bible instead of in front of the tube, or saying no to a temptation when every fiber of your being screams, "Yes!" But the prize is worth the price.

Bodily discipline might help you win a contest, receive admiring glances, or win the heart of an attractive partner. But spiritual discipline that results in spiritual transformation results in a quality of life that begins right now and extends throughout eternity.

As we delve deeper into the process of becoming godly—of reshaping our affections, attitudes, and actions to resemble those of Jesus Christ—we'll look at six heart qualities God wants to develop in each of us: forgiving, obeying, trusting, being content, serving, and praying. Only when we desire, plan, and discipline ourselves to develop these qualities can we cut through the clutter and get to the heart of what God really wants for us.

4

A Forgiving Heart

Clearing Away Anger, Bitterness, and Emotional Knots

Most of us have a love/hate relationship with the subject of forgiveness. We desperately want God to forgive us of our sins, and we assume that He's somehow obligated to do so. Similarly, we expect our family and friends to forgive us when we ignore their feelings, lash out in anger, or violate their trust.

Recently I offended a friend with some pretty strong words about something he'd done. Although I asked him to forgive me, he continues to simmer. I'm more ticked off by his unwillingness to forgive than by the original offense that caused me to speak up. I don't think I'm alone. All of us believe that forgiveness—specifically, people's forgiveness of us—is an unqualified obligation.

We, however, find it difficult to extend the same forgiveness to others that we expect from them...and from God. One study in the *Journal of*

Adult Development found that 75 percent of those surveyed believed that God had forgiven them of past mistakes, but only 52 percent said that they had forgiven other people.[1] Not only do we wrestle with the actual act of forgiving others, but we often find repulsive even the suggestion that we should forgive.

Gerald Ford assumed the presidency in August 1974 when President Richard Nixon was forced to resign. A month later President Ford announced to the nation that he was offering a full pardon to Nixon for crimes committed in the Watergate fiasco, citing the need for the nation to move past Nixon and toward healing. Two years later Ford was defeated in his bid for election in large part because of his decision to pardon Nixon. Many pundits observed that the American people wouldn't forgive Ford for forgiving Nixon.

As C. S. Lewis observed, "Every one says forgiveness is a lovely idea, until they have something to forgive."[2]

Why do we struggle so much with forgiveness? Should we always be forgiving? Are some offenses too heinous to ever be forgiven? What are the consequences of unforgiveness? And can we honestly forgive someone when we don't feel like forgiving?

The Priority of Forgiveness

If God wants us to become like Jesus Christ in our actions, attitudes, and affections, then choosing to forgive those who wrong us is required. Not forgiving is not an option. Jesus placed a high priority on the subject of forgiveness in His teaching. Jesus not only commanded His followers to forgive those who wronged them, but He warned of the dire consequences that await those who refuse to forgive:

For if you forgive men for their transgressions, your heavenly Father will also forgive you. But if you do not forgive men, then your Father will not forgive your transgressions. (Matthew 6:14–15)

And whenever you stand praying, forgive, if you have anything against anyone; so that your Father also who is in heaven may forgive you your transgressions. (Mark 11:25)

But I say to you who hear, love your enemies, do good to those who hate you, bless those who curse you, pray for those who mistreat you. Whoever hits you on the cheek, offer him the other also; and whoever takes away your coat, do not withhold your shirt from him either. (Luke 6:27–29)

You have heard that the ancients were told, "You shall not commit murder" and "Whoever commits murder shall be liable to the court." But I say to you that everyone who is angry with his brother shall be guilty before the court;…and whoever shall say, "You fool," shall be guilty enough to go into the hell of fire. (Matthew 5:21–22)

Actually, some people think that Jesus never intended for us to be able to obey these commands in this life—that these verses describe what life will be like in eternity. Others believe these commands demonstrate how sinful we are by highlighting the great chasm between God's ideal way of living and our natural responses to injustice. Either way, the (mis)application is the same: "Don't worry about trying to do what Jesus instructed in these verses. It's impossible!"

But I believe these commands are more than high-sounding platitudes describing the ideal response to wrong. And I don't think they're simply object lessons demonstrating our need for salvation. How do I know? Because Jesus not only taught forgiveness, He practiced forgiveness. And He expects His followers to do the same. The apostle Peter, describing Jesus's final hours on the cross, wrote:

> Christ also suffered for you, leaving you an example for you
> to follow in His steps, who committed no sin, nor was any
> deceit found in His mouth; and while being reviled, He did
> not revile in return; while suffering, He uttered no threats,
> but kept entrusting Himself to Him who judges righteously.
> (1 Peter 2:21–23)

Jesus's extraordinary forgiveness of those who wronged Him wasn't just a Halley's Comet experience that happens only occasionally. He unconditionally let go of the wrongs committed against Him to teach us how to react to unjust suffering. Apparently, Stephen (the first Christian to die for his faith) learned the lesson well. Look at the way that he followed Jesus's example of forgiveness as he died:

> And they went on stoning Stephen as he called upon the Lord
> and said, "Lord Jesus, receive my spirit!" And falling on his
> knees, he cried out with a loud voice, "Lord, do not hold this
> sin against them!" And having said this, he fell asleep. (Acts
> 7:59–60)

In Stephen's experience we find not just an example of forgiveness, but a definition of forgiveness.

What Is Forgiveness?

Forgiveness is the decision to "not hold this sin against" another person. The word *forgive* means "to let go of, to release, to give up your right to hurt someone else for hurting you." Recently, through studying Jesus's teaching, I've discovered that true forgiveness goes one step further. It actually returns good for evil.

Consider both Jesus's and Stephen's responses to their enemies. Not only did they refuse to threaten those who were killing them, but they actually prayed for God to do something good for their enemies. "Father, forgive them; for they do not know what they are doing" was what Jesus asked of His Father (Luke 23:34). "Lord, do not hold this sin against them!" Stephen interceded for his persecutors (Acts 7:60).

If we have a forgiving heart, we'll genuinely desire good for those who commit evil against us. Jesus commanded, "Bless those who curse you, pray for those who mistreat you" (Luke 6:28). Of course, applying this principle might be difficult when it comes to some offenses. On October 2, 2006, for instance, Charles Carl Roberts entered a one-room schoolhouse in Nickel Mines, Pennsylvania, and shot ten Amish schoolgirls, killing five of them, before turning the gun on himself. Many were dumbfounded by the Amish community's willingness to instantly forgive the murderer and express genuine love for his widow and children. But not everyone was impressed by their demonstration of love. One columnist for the *Boston Globe* wrote, "I admire the Amish villagers' resolve to live up to their Christian ideals even amid heartbreak, but how many of us would really want to live in a society in which no one gets angry when children are slaughtered? In which even the most horrific acts of cruelty were always and instantly forgiven?"[3]

The Root of All Bitterness

Before we discuss how to implement the command to forgive as a way of life, it might be helpful to uncover why forgiveness is a necessary and preferred response to wrong.

A stranger cuts in front of you as you stand in line at the bank, a friend betrays your confidence, your employer refuses to give you a deserved raise, your mate refuses to return your overtures of affection, or a drunk driver takes the life of your child. As different as all of these events are, they elicit exactly the same (though differing in intensity) response from us: anger. In fact, a good definition of *anger* is "a natural physical and emotional reaction to perceived injustice."

A Natural Reaction

When it comes to the reasons we feel emotional steam rising when events like those above occur, it isn't because we're unlike God but because we're like God. We're created in His image. And although that image has been severely tarnished because of sin, every human being—Christian and non-Christian alike—retains a faint resemblance to the Creator. Simply said, the reason we become angry over injustice is because God becomes angry over injustice. Author Gary Chapman, in his book *The Other Side of Love,* points out that the word *anger* appears in the Old Testament 455 times, and 375 of those references are to the anger of God.

In the New Testament, Jesus Christ was not the Casper Milquetoast caricature so often portrayed today. Instead, when He saw the temple being misused as a haven for greed, and when He witnessed the hypocrisy of the Pharisees, He exploded in anger. God hates injustice, and so do we.

Even though our anger is always real, however, it's not always justified. I added the qualifier *perceived* to my definition of anger because sometimes our anger is triggered by information that is either inaccurate or incomplete. I can't count the number of times I've made an angry phone call or written a hot letter to someone over information that later turned out to be inaccurate. Solomon was right: "He who is slow to anger has great understanding, but he who is quick-tempered exalts folly" (Proverbs 14:29).

Other times, our anger can be traced to a violation of an assumed right. For example, church members become angry when there is a change in worship style because they confuse church with Burger King, where you get to "have it your way."

An Emotional Response

In our discussion, however, the key aspect of our definition of anger is that it is a reflexive emotion that always demands a response. Did you know that nowhere in the Bible are we ever commanded not to become angry? To tell someone never to be angry is like ordering someone never to cry or never to laugh. Crying and laughter are physical and emotional responses. They may be inappropriate at certain times, but at other times they are completely justified. Never would we say that at all times crying and laughter are wrong.

The same truth applies to anger. Paul instructed Christians to "be angry, and yet do not sin; do not let the sun go down on your anger" (Ephesians 4:26). Think about that. The Bible never says, "Be greedy and don't sin," or, "Be lustful and don't sin." Greed and lust are always wrong. But anger is an emotion that needs to be managed rather than eliminated from our repertoire of responses.

The Bible, however, notes two natural but ultimately harmful responses to others' wrongdoing: wrath and malice. The word *wrath* comes from the Greek word *thymon,* which can also be translated "rage." Wrath is an immediate, visceral expression of anger. You probably know how it feels to have someone push the right (or, more accurately, wrong) emotional button, causing you to respond with a flood of venomous words that you seemingly have no ability or inclination to stop. We call that "blind rage."

Unfortunately, that kind of rage sometimes doesn't limit itself to words; it can result in violence and even death. An attorney might employ the phrase *temporary insanity* as a defense for a client accused of murdering another person. In a very real sense, rage is a form of insanity, because we surrender control of our behavior to our anger.

However, reason often prevails, and we choose instead to suppress our anger rather than express it. As much as we'd like to slug the employer who insults us or tell off the traffic officer who stops us, good sense rules over our inclination. But that doesn't mean we've managed our anger in a healthy way; it simply means we've buried it.

The Bible calls such buried anger "malice," and it's an embedded, subtle, but very real desire to see our offender suffer. The person who harbors malice will usually take advantage of any opportunity to inflict harm on the offender, perhaps through critical speech or hurtful actions.

This activity is often termed "passive-aggressive behavior." People filled with malice might appear to forgive their offender because they exhibit no outward manifestations of wrath. But deep down, these people wait for the perfect opportunity to get even. The Bible uses the word *bitterness* as a synonym for *malice* and warns against its lethal consequences:

See to it that no one comes short of the grace of God; that no root of bitterness springing up causes trouble, and by it many be defiled. (Hebrews 12:15)

Many people think that if they simply suppress their hostile feelings rather than express them openly, they've forgiven their offender. But the writer of Hebrews described bitterness as a corrosive emotion that eventually destroys the heart where the anger is stored.

Writer Anne Lamott understands the internal damage of unresolved anger. Hear her confession:

> I went around saying for a long time that I am not one of the
> Christians who is heavily into forgiveness—that I am one of the
> other kind. But even though it was funny, and actually true, it
> started to be too painful to stay this way.... In fact, not forgiving
> is like drinking rat poison and waiting for the rat to die.[4]

Suppressed anger does more than harm the person in which it resides. Eventually, bitterness "springs up" and "causes trouble," hurting others as well. Think of suppressed anger as a land mine that remains buried for days, months, or even years. Eventually, some poor, unsuspecting person comes into contact with it, triggering an explosion that results in the destruction of a friendship, a marriage, a congregation, or a community.

Another Option

Beyond reacting in rage or malice, Jesus offered another response to injustice: forgiveness. And forgiveness doesn't mean venting hostile feelings toward another person, rationalizing, "I just thought we needed to clear the air." That is definitely not forgiveness.

We also shouldn't confuse forgiveness with some sort of spiritual sweeping of an injustice under the rug. When people ignore the infidelity of their mate, forget the physical or sexual abuse they endured as a child, or ignore the wounds inflicted by a trusted friend, they are simply burying an emotion that will eventually explode.

True forgiveness is a mechanism we can use to actually diffuse anger rather than express it or bury it. We can even perform this operation by ourselves, without the cooperation of the person who wronged us. Jesus instructed:

> And whenever you stand praying, forgive, if you have anything
> against anyone; so that your Father also who is in heaven may
> forgive you your transgressions. (Mark 11:25)

If you're like me, perhaps your mind tends to wander when you're praying or sitting in a church service (yes, even when I'm preaching, I can be thinking about something else, especially by the second or third service of the day). Whether we're alone praying, in a church service worshiping, or sitting at a stoplight, the natural tendency of our thoughts is to drift toward the offenses others have committed against us. For some masochistic reason, we choose to mentally replay events that have brought so much pain into our lives.

Rather than having us rerun those hurtful episodes in our mind, Jesus encouraged us to rewrite them by changing their ending. Rather than concluding the painful event with "I'll always hate that person," we can choose to say, "I forgive him." The result? By releasing our offender of the wrong, we break the grip bitterness has had on us.

Before we look at how to develop a forgiving heart, let's consider some of the benefits of doing so.

The Benefits of Forgiveness

Remember, heart transformation means that we don't have to wait until we die to experience the benefits of living in the kingdom of God. Although the Almighty has delayed His visible and unopposed rule over the entire earth until a future era, we can choose to submit to His rule right now, and we can begin to experience the benefits of doing so. Submitting to God's rule now includes choosing forgiveness over rage or bitterness—and this isn't an impossible command, especially when we reflect on these practical reasons for doing so.

Settlement of Debt

Forgiveness is often the only transaction capable of settling a debt. In Matthew 18, Jesus told His followers a parable that illustrates the practical benefits of forgiveness. The story concerns a servant who owes a king an incredible amount of money—ten thousand talents. One talent equaled between seventy and eighty pounds of gold. Multiply that by ten thousand and you get an idea of the staggering debt this servant had incurred. To understand how large this debt is, consider that King Herod had a yearly income of nine hundred talents of gold, and the entire regions of Galilee and Perea collected two hundred talents in the year 4 BC. Yet, one slave owed a debt of ten thousand talents! Jesus's listeners got the point. The Lord was saying, "Imagine someone owing a debt that would be impossible to repay in a thousand lifetimes, a debt of gazillions of dollars."

The servant, realizing his financial insolvency and pending punishment, goes to the king to work out an installment plan for repaying the debt. "Have patience with me, and I will repay you everything," he proposes (verse 26). Think about that. This servant owed what conservatively could be estimated at six *billion* dollars at today's gold prices. He probably earned a denarius a day, which, adjusted for inflation, probably meant a salary comparable to that of a day worker, perhaps $25,000 a year. Even if the servant directed all his earnings toward reducing his debt, think how long it would take to eliminate his obligation to the king!

Jesus said that the king, feeling compassion for this slave, "released him and forgave him the debt" (verse 27). Even a hardened monarch couldn't help but be moved by the pitiful sight of this servant promising to pinch and save his denarii so that he could settle a six-billion-dollar debt. Jesus explained that compassion was the king's primary motivation for releasing the slave from his debt.

A more selfish motivation for the king's forgiveness might have been at work here as well, though. Knowing that the servant was incapable of repaying the enormous debt, perhaps the king decided that the only way to settle this debt would be to absorb the loss himself. Why waste valuable time and emotional energy stewing over an account that could never be paid anyway? The king could simply cut his losses and move on with his royal life.

We're wise to follow this king's example when it comes to forgiveness. One reason we hesitate to forgive others is because we mistakenly assume that they can take some action—offer an apology or perhaps some financial restitution—to compensate for the hurt they've inflicted upon us. We fear that if we cancel their debt, we're robbing ourselves of the healing we so desperately crave.

Yet the truth is that our offenders are usually incapable of doing anything to remove or even lessen the hurt they've inflicted upon us. A friend of our family had a stepson who was murdered a number of years ago in a convenience-store robbery in California. The killer was a gang leader who has spent thirty years on death row awaiting his execution. Because of his supposed rehabilitation, though, a number of high-profile citizens petitioned the governor to commute his sentence to life imprisonment. The victim's mother made the rounds on national talk shows and forcefully made her case for the killer's execution.

The governor refused to intervene and invited the mother to California to witness the execution of her son's killer. But even his death was not sufficient to heal the hurt he'd caused. She realized that only forgiveness could erase the debt her offender could never repay.

Freedom from Emotional Bondage

Besides settling an unpayable debt, forgiveness frees us from the emotional bondage that can consume us when someone wrongs us. Most of us understand (even if we don't act on that understanding) the dangers of financial debt. "The borrower becomes the lender's slave," Solomon warned (Proverbs 22:7). But the reverse is true as well: if someone owes you money, you're in bondage to that person until the debt is paid.

I vividly remember the first time I ever cursed. I was in college (honest!), earning some extra income by playing my accordion at weddings, parties, bar mitzvahs…you name it. (Yes, I play the accordion, so go ahead and make your joke now.) A bandleader had hired me to play for a wedding in a town several hours away, and he promised me $65 for the evening. This seemed like a small fortune to a starving college kid. After the evening was over, he explained he didn't have the cash but would mail me a check. Every day for the next several weeks, I went to the mailbox looking for the check. And every day I returned home empty-handed.

I was consumed by his debt. "Is he going to pay?" "Should I sue him?" "What should I have done differently?" Finally, one afternoon I decided to call him. He didn't even pretend that he had ever intended to pay me. He hurled an unprintable insult at me, and in a blind rage I let out an expletive that I had never used before or used since.

A $65 debt had cost me two weeks of my life, not to mention my verbal virginity. Only when I accepted the fact that I'd never be paid was I free to move on with my life.

Whenever someone wrongs you, that person becomes indebted to you—whether or not he or she realizes it. As long as you hold on to that psychological "account receivable," you become emotionally bound to that other person, wondering when and if that debt will ever be satisfied. Forgiveness of your offender's debt is the only way you can ever free yourself and regain control over your life.

I believe the king in Jesus's parable instinctively understood this principle. Sure, he had the right to demand repayment from the slave. Every week, he could have checked with the royal bookkeeper to see if the slave had mailed in his monthly payment as promised. But the king had more important things to do than fret over a debt that could never be satisfied. Rather than being emotionally bound by this uncollectible account, the king chose to cut his losses and move on with his life.

The writer of Hebrews encouraged us to "lay aside every encumbrance, and the sin which so easily entangles us" so that we can "run with endurance the race that is set before us" (12:1). The word *encumbrance* sometimes refers to a debt or mortgage. As long as we hold on to an emotional debt someone owes us for the wrong committed against us, we'll never be free to fulfill God's plan for our lives. Forgiveness is the mechanism we can use to free ourselves from the emotional bondage of bitterness and then move forward.

Assurance of God's Forgiveness

Like so many of Jesus's stories, the parable of the king and the slave has a surprising twist. After being forgiven his enormous debt, the slave remembered a fellow slave who owed him one hundred denarii. Using the above calculations, this would represent about one-third of a laborer's yearly salary, an amount today of about eight thousand dollars. Admittedly, this is no small amount of money, especially for a slave.

The slave grabbed his fellow slave by the throat and began choking him, demanding immediate repayment of the debt. The fellow slave begged for mercy, promising repayment if he could have just a little more time. Unmoved by his plea for mercy, the first slave "threw him in prison until he should pay back what was owed" (Matthew 18:30).

Incensed by what the first slave had done, the king demanded to see him immediately and said:

> You wicked slave, I forgave you all that debt because you entreated
> me. Should you not also have had mercy on your fellow-slave, even
> as I had mercy on you? (verses 32–33)

Why was the king so angry with the slave who refused to forgive a debt? The king never implied that the slave had no legal right to expect repayment of debts owed to him. But the king said the slave had no moral right to insist on repayment, given the tremendous debt from which the king had released him. Compared to six billion dollars, an eight-thousand-dollar debt was relatively insignificant. How could someone who had been forgiven so much refuse to forgive so little?

Notice what happens next in Jesus's story:

> And his lord, moved with anger, handed him over to the torturers
> until he should repay all that was owed him. (verse 34)

Just in case anyone misses the obvious application, Jesus added the final, sobering warning to all of us who struggle with the issue of forgiveness:

> So shall My heavenly Father also do to you, if each of you does not
> forgive his brother from your heart. (verse 35)

Through the years, many people have asked me about this passage: "Does this mean that forgiveness of others is the way I earn God's forgiveness of my sins?" "Is Jesus saying that if I don't forgive another person, I'll lose my salvation?"

We need to be careful not to add or to subtract from Jesus's teaching here. The Lord never taught that we could merit God's forgiveness through any good work, including forgiving others. Nor did Jesus teach that people could lose their salvation through some act of disobedience. Instead, He promised, "I give eternal life to them, and they shall never perish" (John 10:28).

What Jesus meant is simply this. If you find it impossible to forgive others, you haven't really grasped your own need for forgiveness. The debt your offender owes you may be legitimate and large—at least in your own eyes. But compared to the debt you owe God, it's paltry. It's the difference between eight thousand dollars and $16 billion. Only when you truly understand the magnitude of the debt from which God offers to release you, will you be willing to extend the same grace and kindness to others.

Forgiveness is the obligation of the forgiven.

The How-To of Forgiveness

Now that we see the benefits of forgiveness, let's examine the mechanism for forgiving others. How do you develop a forgiving heart? I understand the danger of reducing this important subject into a simple three-step program. Yet, I think a greater danger is to so overanalyze and complicate Jesus's words that we never get around to obeying the command to forgive. So, allow me to offer three suggestions that might help you develop a forgiving heart.

Understand What Forgiveness Is

Forgiveness isn't a feeling. It's a choice. If you wait until an emotional surge of compassion washes over you before you forgive someone, you'll remain a captive to bitterness for a very long time. Reread the climax of Jesus's teaching on forgiveness:

> So shall My heavenly Father also do to you, if each of you does not forgive his brother *from your heart*. (Matthew 18:35)

Admittedly, "from your heart" does sound as if forgiveness is an emotional response…until you recall the Jewish understanding of the heart. In the Jewish worldview, the heart was the center of intellect: "As he thinketh in his heart, so is he" (Proverbs 23:7, KJV).

Doesn't have quite the same effect, does it? Yet by emphasizing the heart as the source of forgiveness, Jesus was teaching His listeners that forgiveness is a conscious action rather than an emotional response.

I can't emphasize this strongly enough. *Forgiveness* isn't a synonym for denying or rationalizing the hurt someone has inflicted upon you. In fact, as one writer points out, it's impossible to forgive those you aren't first willing to blame. When the first servant in Jesus's parable begged for time to repay his loan, the king didn't respond, "Debt? You're mistaken. You don't owe me anything." For any kind of debt to be forgiven, it must first be acknowledged.

Forgiveness begins with the recognition of the offense that someone has committed against you. Forgiveness includes acknowledging the debt someone owes you for an offense, whether that debt involves financial restitution, the dissolution of a relationship, or even imprisonment. Only after this acknowledgment can you choose to release your offender from his or her debt to you—not because you necessarily feel like releasing that person, but because you calculate that the cost of holding on to the debt is more than you're willing to pay.

Realize the Consequences of Unforgiveness

One of the strongest motivations for forgiving is realizing what forgiveness does for you. Some Christians choke on this statement because of a fundamentally mistaken notion that our obedience to Christ should never be based on personal benefit. Yet, as we've discussed several times, submitting to the rule of Christ over our hearts allows us to experience the benefits of living in the kingdom of God now, not just in eternity.

As you carefully read Jesus's parable about forgiveness, you see a vivid illustration of the cost of unforgiveness. Because the unforgiving slave refused to let go of a relatively paltry debt, he was placed in prison where he was tortured day and night.

Choosing to hold on to an offender's debt rather than forgiving it places us in a prison of resentment. The word *resentment* means "to feel again." Every time you relive someone's offense against you instead of releasing it, *you*—not your offender—experience the wound again. Only the most hard-core masochists would ever choose to allow someone to torture them again and again.

Forgiveness is the only way to separate yourself from the pain of resentment. As the late Lewis Smedes observed, "The first and often the only person to be healed by forgiveness is the person who does the forgiving.... When we genuinely forgive, we set a prisoner free and then discover that the prisoner we set free was us."[5]

Of course, we must also weigh the eternal cost of unforgiveness. Jesus said it very simply: if you won't forgive others, God won't forgive you. As author George Herbert wrote, "He who cannot forgive another breaks the bridge over which he must pass himself."[6] That realization alone is the greatest motivation for choosing forgiveness over resentment.

Return Good for Evil

Jesus went one step further after commanding us to let go of offenses, providing us with a final principle for forgiving: do something beneficial for those who wrong you. Jesus said:

> Love your enemies, do good to those you hate you, bless those you curse you, pray for those who mistreat you. (Luke 6:27–28)

Frankly, words like these cause many Christians to conclude that Jesus's commands are unreasonable and impossible to keep. Yet I believe that with these words Jesus provides us with a way to develop a forgiving heart.

You see, simply put, it's impossible to both hate and pray for someone at the same time. Of course, loving and praying for your enemies doesn't mean loving the wrong they have committed against you. Nor does loving and praying for them require you to develop a relationship with your offenders.

Instead, loving your enemies simply means desiring God's best for them, which certainly includes desiring their reconciliation with God. As the fourth-century church leader Chrysostom said, "A wrong done against love is like a spark that falls into the sea and is quenched." Praying for and desiring God's best for your enemy is the only way to extinguish the burning ember of resentment in your heart.

The story of Paige McKenzie, a political aide to a New Mexico gubernatorial candidate, provides an amazing example of returning good for evil. McKenzie had stopped in a bank parking lot to change a flat tire. There, an unknown assailant attacked her, resulting in a broken jaw, several other broken bones, and splintered teeth. McKenzie underwent several surgeries and now wears a permanent chin plate.

In a newspaper interview, McKenzie claimed that it was her faith that sustained her during the attack and motivated her to pray for her assailant. "I just want him to know that Christ loves him and wants to forgive him. I can't imagine how anyone that miserable can go through life with so much hatred."[7] "Father, forgive them; for they know not what they do," Jesus cried out on behalf of those who crucified Him (Luke 23:34, KJV). In doing so, He left for us an example to follow. As one wise person observed, "We are most like beasts when we kill. We are most like men when we judge. We are most like Christ when we forgive."[8]

An Obeying Heart

Saying Yes to the Impossible

I'm not a tyrannical despot, but I do like people who obey me. I appreciate those under my authority who do what I ask them to do without a lot of resistance.

We recently hired someone to paint the exterior of our home. Every simple suggestion I made was met with a dozen reasons why he wouldn't or couldn't do as I requested. Apparently, the concept that the customer is always right—or even sometimes right—was unfamiliar to him. At the outset of the project, my wife and I had had great hopes for all the tasks we'd like him to do for us in the future. But after this unpleasant experience, we'll never hire him again for anything. He never accepted the nature of the relationship; he had trouble remembering who worked for whom.

When I ask my staff members to either do something or refrain from doing something, it's usually because I have a better grasp of the overall condition of our organization than they do. Even though the staff members may not understand exactly why my request is important—and sometimes I'm not free to share all the information I have—it's refreshing when they acquiesce out of their faith in my leadership ability. Call it favoritism (and some people do), but those are the staff members who receive raises and promotions.

Many years ago, when Dr. James Dobson wrote a book contrasting a strong-willed child and a compliant child, I wondered how and when he'd met my two daughters. Whenever I ask one to do something, she almost immediately responds, "Yes, Daddy." For my other child, the default response is, "You've got to be kidding!" Although we may love our children equally, we tend to favor the child who obeys our requests.

Just recently I had a serious discussion with one of my daughters about something she was doing. I explained the dangers involved and asked her to promise me that she'd stop. "Honey, I love you, and I only want the best for you," I said after I'd stated my case. I wasn't sure what her reaction would be, but I was relieved when tears started streaming down her face and she said, "I know," and she promised to do what I asked. At that moment, I would have done anything for her.

The reason I tend to choose to use, reward, and favor those who follow my leadership is because I'm made in God's image. God Himself uses, rewards, and favors those of His children who obey Him because they

- understand the nature of their relationship with Him
- respect His judgment
- trust His motives
- love Him

What does God really want from me? My immediate, complete, joyful, and loving obedience to His commands. The word *obedience* doesn't require a great deal of explanation. To obey God means to do what He asks us to do. We've already seen the premium that Jesus placed on obedience:

He who has My commandments and keeps them, he it is who loves Me; and he who loves Me shall be loved by My Father, and I will love him, and will disclose Myself to him. (John 14:21)

Truly, truly, I say to you, if anyone keeps My word he shall never see death. (John 8:51)

He who believes in the Son has eternal life; but he who does not obey the Son shall not see life, but the wrath of God abides on him. (John 3:36)

Many Christians struggle with the tension between belief and obedience, subtly thinking that belief in Christ is essential but obedience to Christ is optional. These folks trust God to take care of them in the next life, yet they apparently don't trust Him enough to obey Him in this one.

Yet the words about and from Jesus that we just read don't allow for such a dichotomy. Most evangelical Christians would agree that we're saved by trusting in Christ's death on the cross for the atonement of our sins. But, as New Testament scholar W. E. Vine points out, the similarity between the two Greek words for obey (*peithō*) and trust (*pistueo*) aren't accidental:

When a man obeys God he gives the only possible evidence that in his heart he believes God.... Peithō ["obey"] in the N.T. suggests an actual and outward result of the inward persuasion and consequent faith.[1]

The words *believe* and *obey* are used interchangeably in John 3:36. The person who *believes* in Christ will have eternal life. But those who don't *obey* the Son do not have eternal life, because their lack of obedience indicates their lack of belief. According to the One who best understands what God really wants from us, to believe without obeying isn't really to believe at all.

Jesus not only commanded obedience, but He demonstrated it in His own life. Jesus was consumed with a passion to obey God:

> My food is to do the will of Him who sent Me, and to accomplish His work. (John 4:34)

> For I have come down from heaven, not to do My own will, but the will of Him who sent Me. (John 6:38)

The Obedience God Desires

Stop here for a moment and ask yourself this simple question: is the driving passion of your life the desire to do what God asks you to do? Be honest. When you awaken in the morning, is your first thought, "How would God have me spend my time today?"? Before you drift off to sleep at night, is your final thought, "I hope God was pleased with me today"?

Jesus not only talked about obedience, but He demonstrated three important facets of the kind of obedience that God desires from us.

Immediate Obedience
I'm not suggesting that Jesus didn't struggle with the cost of obeying God. He wasn't a heavenly robot programmed to say, "Yes sir," the moment God the Father issued an edict. Jesus was fully human as well as fully divine, which means He experienced the same difficulties with obedience that you and I do.

Case in point. From the beginning of His life, Jesus understood that His mission was "to give His life a ransom for many" (Mark 10:45). That was the Father's plan. Still, the night before He was to die, Jesus wrestled with God's will. He cried out in Gethsemane, "Father, if Thou art willing, remove this cup from Me" (Luke 22:42). Yes, Jesus experienced a moment of struggle—but it was only a moment as almost immediately Jesus added, "Yet not My will, but Thine be done."

My former seminary professor Haddon Robinson poses the question:

Where was it that Jesus sweat great drops of blood? Not in Pilate's Hall, nor on his way to Golgotha. It was in the Garden of Gethsemane. There he "offered up prayers and petitions with loud cries and tears to the One who could save him from death" (Hebrews 5:7). Had I been there and witnessed that struggle, I would have worried about the future. "If he is so broken up when all he is doing is praying," I might have said, "what will he do when he faces a real crisis? Why can't he approach this ordeal with the calm confidence of his three sleeping friends?" Yet, when the test came, Jesus walked to the cross with courage, and his three friends fell apart and fell away.[2]

Jesus's conflicting emotions concerning God's clearly stated plan were normal. Still, the struggle didn't last for days, weeks, or months. It was settled in a matter of moments. "Not My will, but Your will be done," Jesus stated.

Complete Obedience

The Puritan writer Thomas Brooks observed, "No man obeys God truly who does not endeavor to obey God fully." Many times we approach obedience like a menu handed to us in a restaurant: we choose only those items that are pleasing to us. But Jesus didn't practice selective obedience. Instead, as Paul described, Jesus was "obedient to the point of death, even death on a cross" (Philippians 2:8).

Jesus's obedience knew no limits, and God desires the same from each of us. According to Jesus, the very definition of a disciple is one who observes "*all* things whatsoever I have commanded" (Matthew 28:20, KJV).

Sometimes we read the stories in the Old Testament and can't help but question the severity of God's judgment against what seem insignificant transgressions:

- Achan kept a few spoils of victory, which led to the defeat of Israel at Ai.
- Saul decided to spare a couple of sheep from slaughter, which led to his removal as king.
- The man who touched the Ark of the Covenant in a sincere desire to keep it from falling was struck dead.

These incidents, however, demonstrate that the kind of obedience God desires from each of us is total, not partial.

Perhaps you feel that you've completely devoted your life to following Christ. You've surrendered every area of your life to His control…except one. An immoral habit, a wrong relationship, or even an unsurrendered dream might be a spoil of victory over which you're retaining control. Only when you're willing to submit to God's rule over *every* aspect of your life will your obedience mirror that of Christ's.

Joyful Obedience

Since the parent-child relationship is one of the most frequent metaphors in the Bible for God's relationship with us, let's use to it to understand another aspect of the kind of obedience God desires.

Imagine that you're entertaining friends in your home. During the course of the evening, you ask your child to empty the trash. After you spend ten minutes asking and arguing, cajoling and threatening, he finally gives in but stomps around the house emitting those clearly audible grunts and groans as your guests look on.

How do you feel? While he might deserve some credit for doing what you asked, the whole ordeal has embarrassed you in front of your friends. Wouldn't you prefer a simple "Yes ma'am," followed by immediate and quiet compliance?

I'm not suggesting that God expects us to be giddy over every command He issues. But once we settle the initial struggle in our own spirit, we obey without resistance, believing that God will reward our efforts. That kind of obedience glorifies our heavenly Father in front of those on earth as well as the unseen audience in heaven. John Piper explains how joyful obedience enhances God's reputation both on earth and in heaven:

> God's deepest purpose for the world is to fill it with reverberations of his glory in the lives of a new humanity, ransomed from every people, tribe, tongue, and nation (Rev. 5:9). But the glory of God does not reflect brightly in the hearts of men and women when they cower unwillingly in submission to his authority or when they obey in servile fear or when there is no gladness in their response to the glory of their King....
>
> [God's] aim is not to constrain man's submission by an act of raw authority; his aim is to ravish their affections with irresistible displays of glory. The only submission that fully reflects the worth and glory of the King is glad submission.... No gladness in the subject, no glory to the King.[3]

The writer of Hebrews used the analogy of an Olympic-style race to describe our brief experience on earth. The stadium is packed with "a cloud of witnesses surrounding us" and watching us as we run the course that God sets before us (12:1). The race is not easy. Finishing requires an extraordinary amount of perspiration and determination. But just when we want to give up, God encourages us to look up to the inspiration He provided, to Someone like us who completed the even more difficult course that was set before Him:

> Fixing our eyes on Jesus, the author and perfecter of faith, who for
> the joy set before Him endured the cross. (verse 2)

No, Jesus wasn't ecstatic over the idea of crucifixion. Who would be? But as the audience on earth and in heaven watched, Jesus obeyed His Father's command without resistance, because He looked beyond the immediate agony of Calvary to the ecstasy of God's unending reward.

Barriers to Our Obedience

If we believe that God will ultimately reward our obedience, what prevents us from the immediate, total, and joyful obedience that God desires from us? I can think of at least two primary doubts we face that act as barriers.

Is God Relevant?

This past year our family experienced a milestone event: our older daughter moved out of our home to go to college. Granted, she didn't move far—about a mile down the road into a house with three other girls. Still, the event was traumatic—not for her, but for us. We've attempted to respect her privacy and her need to feel as if she's on her own by resisting the urge to drop in when we're in the neighborhood (which is just about every day).

In fact, the only time I'd been in her house was the day she moved in about eight months ago.

But she recently needed some help moving furniture, and I gladly agreed to assist. When I walked into her room, I noticed dozens of photographs on her bulletin boards, her desk, and her bedside table. Pictures of her and her sister, her and her best friends, her and her sorority sisters, and her and her boyfriend—lots of those.

But I couldn't find any pictures of my daughter with the person I thought should be the most important person in her life! Why not? My daughter certainly believes I'm alive (as evidenced by her constant requests for money). I have no doubt that she loves me: she calls me several times a day to ask for advice or tell me about something that happened. But the physical distance between us has diminished my relevance in her life. Out of sight, out of mind.

Could that same phenomenon explain why obedience to our heavenly Father isn't the predominant passion in our lives? We haven't stopped believing in the reality of God, but we no longer embrace the relevance of God. If you balk at such a claim, ask yourself how long you're able to go without even thinking about God, much less worshiping, reading about, or praying to Him. Minutes? Hours? Days? Longer?

Frankly, obeying an invisible God has always been challenging. Remember the account of the Israelites' gross disobedience at the foot of Mount Sinai (Exodus 32)? Their leader Moses ascended the mountain to meet with God and receive the Law. Not having expected Moses to be gone for more than a month, the people became restless. It was hard enough to march around in the wilderness following an invisible God, but when it seemed that their visible leader had been vaporized, it was too much:

Come, make us a god who will go before us; as for this Moses, the man who brought us up from the land of Egypt, we do not know what has become of him. (verse 1)

This event marked the start of the Israelites' descent into idolatry, immorality, and rebellion, which eventually prevented this generation from entering the Promised Land. Again, whether we're talking about Moses or Jehovah, the principle was the same: out of sight, out of mind.

In a similar way, the rampant disobedience that will permeate the world in the last days is attributable to the lack of Christ's visible presence. The apostle Peter wrote:

Know this first of all, that in the last days mockers will come with their mocking, following after their own lusts, and saying, "Where is the promise of His coming? For ever since the fathers fell asleep, all continues just as it was from the beginning of creation." (2 Peter 3:3–4)

While the physical and spiritual distance between finite creatures and their infinite Creator is a logical explanation for the difficulty of obedience, that distance is not an acceptable excuse for disobedience.

Do We Trust God?

Perhaps an even greater barrier to our obeying God is our innate distrust of Him. Few of us have difficulty believing that God is wiser than we are. After all, He's been around longer than we have. Furthermore, His ability to know the past and see into the future provides Him with a better perspective on life and eternity. It only makes sense that God knows better than we do what is good for us and what hurts us. So why do we find it so difficult to do what He says?

Because, in the deepest recesses of our heart, we don't trust God's motives. The words Satan whispered into Eve's ear continue to reverberate in ours: *God prohibits to inhibit your happiness.* This basic distrust of God's character, planted in Eve's heart, resides in every human heart today.

As I was writing this paragraph, my cell phone rang. The repairman at our automotive shop was calling to deliver some bad news. The reason my car was losing coolant wasn't a ruptured hose, as he first thought, but an engine gasket that needed to be retooled. The cost for fixing the car would be thirteen hundred dollars instead of the original estimate of one hundred.

I have no doubt that the repairman knows more about cars than I do, but I'm not sure about his motives. How do I know he's telling the truth and really trying to help me instead of simply wanting to line his own pockets? Only after I call around to verify his character will I be willing to trust him.

The same dynamic applies in our relationship with God. Someone said, "All sin is contempt for God." When we fail to follow God's commands (He doesn't make suggestions), we cast a vote of no confidence in His character. Only when we're convinced of God's trustworthiness will we be motivated to follow His commands.

Developing an Obedient Heart

Even for the most well-intentioned Christian, obedience isn't an automatic impulse. Instead, it's a learned behavior. The Bible tells us that even Jesus Himself—the perfect Son of God—had to "[learn] obedience" (Hebrews 5:8). The mandate Christ gave us was to "[teach] them to observe all things whatsoever I have commanded you" (Matthew 28:20, KJV).

How do we learn to obey? I believe at least four principles are essential to developing an obedient heart.

Decide That Obedience Is a Priority

This principle seems so obvious that I hesitate to mention it. Yet making obedience to God a priority is foundational to the process of spiritual transformation. To put it bluntly, the reason most of us don't obey God is because we don't intend to obey God. William Law explained this idea more fully:

> It is purely for want of this degree of piety that you see such a mixture of sin and folly in the lives even of the better sort of people.... It was this general intention that made the primitive Christians such eminent instances of piety...and if you will here stop and ask yourself why you are not as pious as the primitive Christians were, your own heart will tell you that is neither through ignorance nor inability, but purely because you never thoroughly intended it.[4]

I don't mean to suggest that making some one-time decision can forever end our struggle to obey God. But I do believe we must settle the issue in our own mind regarding the character of God. Can He be trusted? Does He really want what's best for me? Does He really *know* what's best for me?

A number of years ago I went to a gastroenterologist for some advice. My mother had died of colon cancer at a very early age. Knowing that this disease is largely related to lifestyle choices, I wanted some expert advice on how to avoid it. After drawing a detailed sketch of the upper intestine and lower intestine and explaining the digestive process in graphic detail, the doctor offered this advice: "Eat a bowl of bran flakes sprinkled with unprocessed wheat bran every morning for breakfast, and drink a glass of Metamucil each evening before you go to bed." That simple advice cost me $120.00!

Still, I've followed my doctor's advice for the last fifteen years, and… well, I won't go into any more detail. Why was I willing to fork over hard-earned cash for that simple counsel? Because I believe my doctor knows more than I do about staying healthy. And why do I gag down my high-fiber cereal in the morning and a high-fiber drink at night? Not because it's pleasant. A sausage biscuit from McDonald's for breakfast and a chocolate milkshake before bedtime would be much more enjoyable. But I follow my doctor's directions because I believe he wants what's best for me.

You'll never obey God consistently without first *intending* to obey God. And developing the intention to obey God begins with the conviction that you can trust God's character and that obeying His commands will result in a better life. I encourage you to memorize and reflect on this passage from Psalm 19 to remind yourself of the wisdom and goodness of God:

> The law of the LORD is perfect, restoring the soul;
> The testimony of the LORD is sure, making wise the simple.
> The precepts of the LORD are right, rejoicing the heart;
> The commandment of the LORD is pure, enlightening the eyes.
> The fear of the LORD is clean, enduring forever;
> The judgments of the LORD are true; they are righteous altogether.
> They are more desirable than gold, yes, than much fine gold;
> Sweeter also than honey and the drippings of the honeycomb.
> (verses 7–10)

Develop a "God Is Here" Mind-Set

Intending to keep God's commands is essential but not sufficient for developing an obedient heart. We also need to be aware of God's constant presence in our lives.

Remember my earlier story about the pictures in my daughter's bedroom? Out of sight, out of mind. But imagine if she put up on the wall opposite her bed a life-size poster of me holding an open Bible in one hand and pointing at her with the other. The first thing she'd see when she awakened every morning and the last thing she'd see before she went to bed every night would be dear old Dad. Such an image wouldn't automatically cause her to live the way I want her to live, but at least it would remind her of me and some of the things I've said to her in the past.

We need a way to be reminded of God's presence in our lives, and King David shows us how. With one simple phrase, David provides invaluable insight into how he became a man after God's own heart. Sure, he suffered relapses in his relationship with the Lord, but the general direction of his life was toward God rather than away from God. What was David's secret?

> I have set the LORD continually before me;
> Because He is at my right hand, I will not be shaken. (Psalm 16:8)

Of course, the omnipresent God is always before us, behind us, and all around us. "Where can I go from Thy Spirit?" David wrote in Psalm 139:7. But that theological reality didn't automatically translate into David's practical awareness of God's continual presence. Like all of us, David experienced the challenge of serving an invisible God, so he developed a way to "set the LORD continually before [him]." How did David constantly remind himself of the reality and presence of God?

First, the psalms reveal that David meditated on God's Word continually. I'll confess that at times (more often than I care to admit), my daily reading of God's Word tastes more like bran flakes with no milk than the "drippings of the honeycomb" that David described. But as dry as the experience might be, my reading of God's Word at the very least reminds me that there is a God in whom we "live, and move, and have our being" (Acts 17:28, KJV).

Additionally, since we know that David comforted King Saul by the playing of his harp, we can assume music was instrumental (pardon the pun) in his own worship. Music can be a powerful reminder of God's desires for our life. The other day the seven-year-old girl my older daughter watches as a part-time job completely ruined the backseat of my daughter's car with a dripping Popsicle. To make matters worse, she showed no remorse at all. Infuriated, my daughter was about to unload on the girl when the song "Amazing Grace" came on the radio. She said it was as if God were speaking to her, reminding her that if she expected to receive grace, she needed to extend it as well.

Beyond a regular intake of God's Word and listening to inspirational music, you might use other creative methods to "set the Lord" before you. Hanging plaques with Scripture verses in your home or office, keeping on your desk pictures or mementos representing spiritual milestones in your life (baptism, a conference, a retreat), or listening to sermons or Christian teaching while you're exercising or running errands in the car are all ways to keep God part of your daily life.

An inseparable connection exists between thinking about God and obeying Him. A missionary and pioneer in the field of adult literacy, Frank Laubach spent his life developing the habit of constantly thinking about God. He played what he called "games with minutes" seeing how quickly he could redirect his thoughts toward God. Laubach understood that thoughts about God were key in surrendering to God:

As for me, I never lived, I was half dead, I was a rotting tree, until I reached the place where I wholly, with utter honesty, resolved and then re-resolved that I *would* find God's will, and I *would* do that will though every fibre in me said no, and I *would* win the battle in my thoughts. It was as though some deep artesian well had been struck in my soul....

Money, praise, poverty, opposition, these make no difference, for they will all alike be forgotten in a thousand years, but this spirit which comes to a mind set upon continuous surrender, this spirit is timeless life.[5]

Obey What You Know to Be True

Let's return to the physician-patient analogy for a moment. Suppose you go to your doctor complaining of shortness of breath and chronic fatigue. A battery of tests reveals that your arteries have accumulated a significant amount of plaque, your cholesterol is through the roof, and your heart muscle is weak. You doctor prescribes a low-fat diet, a vigorous exercise program, and medication to reduce your cholesterol.

At first you agree to do anything and everything necessary to regain your health. But after a week you decide that you don't have time to exercise and the low-fat diet is just too difficult to maintain. But you can pop a pill once a day to reduce your cholesterol.

What would be the result of your decision? Certainly you'd be in better shape than if you ignored all of your doctor's orders. But your selective compliance with your doctor's advice has two destructive consequences—one that is obvious and another that's not so clear.

First, refusing to comply with the doctor's exercise and dietary suggestions robs you of the health benefits each provides. That's the obvious destructive consequence. The less obvious consequence of your selective obedience to your doctor's wishes is the reinforcement of a behavioral pattern that could ultimately be disastrous. If you can ignore two of his three suggestions for restoring your health, what will prevent you from ignoring his third suggestion if, for example, the medication becomes too expensive or produces some unpleasant side effects? What if one day your doctor decides you need an operation to clear out your clogged arteries? Will you decide to ignore that advice as well? Do you have the necessary medical expertise to determine which orders are essential and which are optional?

Selective obedience to God's commands entails the same risks. When we blatantly ignore what we know to be God's will for our lives, we cultivate a habit of disobedience that eventually becomes the rule rather than the exception in our lives. Perhaps that realization is behind Oswald Chambers's counsel:

> Obey God in the thing he shows you, and instantly the next thing
> is opened up. God will never reveal more truth about himself until
> you have obeyed what you know already.[6]

Although many Christians see selective obedience as a viable option, God demands complete adherence to His commands:

> Obey Him with *all* your heart and soul according to *all* that I com-
> mand you today, you and your sons. (Deuteronomy 30:2)

> Take to your heart *all* the words with which I am warning you
> today, which you shall command your sons to observe carefully,
> even *all* the words of this law. (Deuteronomy 32:46)

> Oh that my ways may be established
> To keep Thy statutes!

Then I shall not be ashamed
When I look upon all Thy commandments. (Psalm 119:5–6)

Are you obeying *all* of God's commands? Or in certain areas of your life do you find yourself practicing selective obedience? The only way to make obedience a habit is to obey all that you know to be true.

Remember the Reward for Obedience

Finally, you can develop an obedient heart when you're convinced that God exists and that He rewards those who obey Him. The author of Hebrews explained:

And without faith it is impossible to please Him, for he who comes
to God must believe that He is, and that He is a rewarder of those
who seek Him. (11:6)

Believing in the invisible God's existence is an obvious prerequisite for obeying Him. For example, if I didn't believe that state troopers lurked behind trees or waited over the next hill with radar guns, my driving habits would change considerably. I might not speed all of the time, but I'd exceed the posted limits more often than I do now.

Still, a belief in the reality of God isn't enough to sustain consistent obedience to Him. We must also believe that a payoff for submitting to His commands will come somewhere at some time.

In our culture we tend to think of rewards as an inferior motivation for obedience. We fear that parents who reward their children with money for performing household chores or that the first-grade teacher who distributes candy for good behavior sets a dangerous precedent. We should learn to do the right thing because...well, it's the right thing to do!

But God has a different idea. He not only wants us to believe in rewards. In fact, He demands it. As the author of Hebrews wrote, we "must believe...that He is a rewarder" (11:6). Why? Because without the assurance of some kind of reward, we'll find it difficult to:

- stay in a troubled marriage
- refrain from an immoral, but pleasurable activity
- remain in a difficult ministry
- give away our financial resources

Read the remainder of Hebrews 11 and you'll discover men and women who obeyed God for one reason: they were "looking to the reward" (verse 26). Some, like Noah, experienced immediate benefits for their obedience (like not drowning). Others, like Moses, died without seeing any reward for following God. But none of those mentioned received the *full* reward in this life.

All these died in faith, without receiving the promises, but having seen them and having welcomed them from a distance, and having confessed that they were strangers and exiles on the earth.... But as it is, they desire a better country, that is a heavenly one. (verses 13, 16)

Each of these individuals lived and died believing that God would one day reward their obedience. The ultimate example of obedience is Jesus Himself, "the author and perfecter of faith, who for the joy set before Him endured the cross, despising the shame, and has sat down at the right hand of the throne of God" (Hebrews 12:2).

What was Jesus's motivation? Why did He choose to endure the excruciating experience of the Cross? "The joy set before him" was the reason. Jesus's unwavering conviction that God would reward Him with a name above every name and a place at His Father's right hand sustained Him through the ordeal of the cross.

No act of obedience—no matter how small—is inconsequential or unnoticed. Whether it's saying no to some momentary temptation or saying yes when asked to make the ultimate sacrifice, God sees every act, and one day He will reward them.

Author Philip Yancey illustrates this when he tells about watching a documentary on some of the survivors of World War II:

> The soldiers recalled how they spent a particular day. One sat in a foxhole all day; once or twice, a German tank drove by, and he shot at it. Others played cards and frittered away the time. A few got involved in furious firefights. Mostly, the day passed like any other day for an infantryman on the front. Later, they learned they had just participated in one of the largest, most decisive engagements of the war, the Battle of the Bulge. It did not *feel* decisive to any of them at the time, because none had the big picture of what was happening elsewhere.
>
> Great victories are won when ordinary people execute their assigned tasks—and a faithful person does not debate each day whether he or she is in the mood to follow the sergeant's orders or show up at a boring job. We exercise faith by responding to the task that lies before us, for we have control only over our actions in the present moment.[7]

What is God asking you to do in this present moment? In what area is He asking you to obey Him? It might be monumental. Or it might seem inconsequential. But saying, "Yes, Lord," is your first step in developing an obedient heart.

A Trusting Heart

Allowing Peace to Rule Your Life

I'm looking for a volunteer who will help me this morning," I said at the beginning of a message. I scanned the congregation, looking for a responsive face. Realizing that no one was too eager to subject themselves to a potentially embarrassing situation in front of a large crowd and television cameras, I selected a middle-aged woman and asked her to come forward.

"I'm going to make you a promise: whatever happens in these next few moments, if you do what I ask you to do, you'll leave here better off than you are now. Do you believe me?"

She nodded her head affirmatively but tentatively as the congregation registered its own doubts through muffled giggles.

"I'm going to ask you for some things that you have. If you give them to me, they're mine forever, and I can do whatever I want with them. Do you understand?"

"Yes."

"I see you brought your purse with you today. Do you have a wallet in your purse?"

"Yes," she replied, very unsure about where this was going.

"How much money do you have in your wallet?"

She opened it and pulled out twenty-three dollars.

"May I have that?" I asked.

"Sure," she said, forking over the cash.

"That's a beautiful watch you have. Any idea how much that cost?"

"No, I just know it was expensive."

"My wife would certainly enjoy a watch like that," I mused. The crowd began laughing.

"May I have that watch?"

She hesitated.

"Remember, if you give it to me, it's mine forever. But remember my promise that if you do what I ask, you'll be better off than when you came up on the stage."

Reluctantly, she removed the watch and handed it to me.

"Wow, that wedding ring is really something! Your husband must love you a lot to give you something like that!!" The crowd roared with laughter.

Now, I imagined that when I asked for her wedding ring, she'd respond, "No way!" After all, that's what happened when I saw another pastor use this illustration. But to my surprise, she slipped off her ring and handed it to me.

"Are you and Bill having some problems in your relationship that you want to confess right now?" Everyone laughed even harder.

"No," my volunteer responded. "But you said that if I give you everything you ask for, I'll be better off than when I came up here. And I trust you."

Astounded, I took the ring and placed it in my pocket along with the other items. Then I said, "All these things you've given me are mine now. But, truthfully, I have no need of twenty-three dollars, a watch, or a wedding ring. So I'm returning them to you. But I also promised that you'd leave the platform better off than before."

Reaching into my pocket, I pulled out a crisp fifty-dollar bill and said, "Take your husband to lunch today on me—since you and Bill obviously need to work on your relationship!"

Unlike this woman, most people would limit what they were willing to give me because of their lack of faith in either my desire or my ability to keep my promise. What could I possibly give them to compensate for an expensive watch or a treasured wedding ring?

Similarly, God promises that those who follow His commands will be better off than those who don't. And we believe Him...up to a point. We're usually willing to refrain from committing the really big sins such as murder or embezzlement, realizing that the potential consequences outweigh the benefits. Or we obey in a particular area of life because we're not inclined, or we don't have the opportunity, to disobey God.

But when God asks us either to surrender something we value or to refrain from an experience we desire, suddenly we're confronted with a difficult choice. Even though God promises that those who obey Him will be better off than those who don't, can we really trust God to keep His promise?

We cannot practice the immediate, total, and joyful obedience described in the preceding chapter until we first develop a trusting heart.

The Importance of Faith

The Bible often uses the word *faith* as a synonym for *trust*. Throughout both the Old and New Testaments, God places a premium on faith:

The righteous will live by his faith. (Habakkuk 2:4)

For truly I say to you, if you have faith as a mustard seed, you shall say to this mountain, "Move from here to there," and it shall move; and nothing shall be impossible to you. (Matthew 17:20)

And seeing their faith, He said, "Friend, your sins are forgiven you." (Luke 5:20)

And He said to the woman, "Your faith has saved you; go in peace." (Luke 7:50)

And without faith it is impossible to please Him. (Hebrews 11:6)

If we want to exercise the kind of faith that God desires, it's important to understand what faith is…and what it's not. Faith isn't the ability to predict the outcome of future circumstances. "I'm trusting God for that job"; "I'm trusting God that my marriage will be restored"; "I'm trusting God that my child will be healed"—such grandiose statements aren't faith, but presumption.

Unless God has audibly communicated to you that He's going to act in these situations, what would lead you to think they're actually going to happen the way you want, hope, or expect? Do we really think that God can be manipulated into acting in a certain way by the strength of our willpower? Would we really want to serve a God who was nothing more than a divine errand boy making Himself available to do our bidding?

At the same time, faith is not the complete absence of any doubt. Last year I led a tour to Greece and Turkey that traced Paul's second missionary journey. I had faith in the airline pilot to land our plane safely at our destination. I had faith that the captain of our ship wouldn't capsize the boat. I had faith that counterterrorism officials would successfully thwart any plot that might endanger our lives.

However, before we departed, I called my best friend and provided him with a list of instructions of what to do for my wife and children in case something did happen. If I'd been 100 percent certain of our safe return, I wouldn't have wasted the time. But I had enough faith in the pilot, the captain, and the government officials—none of whom I'd ever met—to make the trip.

God isn't concerned about the quantity of our faith. Jesus Himself observed that even faith the size of a mustard seed—one of the smallest seeds in the vegetable world—can produce great results. For example, although the woman I described at the beginning of this chapter gave me her wedding ring, I imagine she still harbored some doubt about the outcome of her actions. Yet, in spite of her doubts, she chose to give me the ring, and so she experienced the benefits of trusting me and acting in faith.

Similarly, the kind of faith that God desires from us doesn't require us to rid ourselves of all uncertainty before we obey Him. All we need is just enough faith to act, and then we'll enjoy the benefits of God's promises.

I define *faith* as follows:

> Faith is believing that God will do what
> He has promised…and acting accordingly.

As I demonstrated to my congregation, trust lies at the heart of obedience. I asked the woman why she was willing to give me her wedding ring. "Because you promised I'd be better off if I did, and I *trusted* you," she responded. Before we can obey God, we must believe that He has both the ability and the character to fulfill His promises. Acting on that belief requires us to have a trusting heart.

As a father, I've always wanted my daughters to trust me. Even though they might not understand or agree with me, I want them to have faith in my judgment when I ask them to refrain from certain actions, believing that I truly desire what's best for them. When they run into a problem that overwhelms them, I want them to trust my love for them so that they'll come to me. When they're anxious about their future, I want them to trust in my ability and willingness to provide for their needs. Is it any surprise that our heavenly Father wants us to show the same kind of trust in Him?

A Trusting Heart

In the remainder of this chapter I want to define a trusting heart as:

> Allowing our confidence in God's character to govern
> our inward emotions and our outward behavior.

Consider the life of Jesus Christ. At the heart of His complete obedience to God and the lack of inward turmoil in His life was His complete confidence in God's character, God's love, God's wisdom, and God's power. Jesus refused to allow outward circumstances to extinguish His inward peace, and God desires the same for you. The apostle Paul encouraged us to:

Let the peace of Christ rule in your hearts. (Colossians 3:15)

I want you to grasp two important concepts in this command. Let's briefly examine each one.

The Peace of Christ

First, we need to understand what Paul meant by "the peace of Christ." The word *peace* means "absence of turmoil or hostility." Earlier in Colossians 3, Paul commanded believers to lay aside acts of disobedience that result from inner turmoil such as "immorality, impurity, passion, evil desire, and greed" (verse 5). The reason people chase after new sexual experiences and more money is because they lack the inner peace that comes from trusting God with their wants and needs.

Likewise, the second list of negative behaviors, mentioned in verse 8, results from inner hostility: "anger, wrath, malice, slander, and abusive speech." At the heart of hostility toward others is the belief that other people control our lives and are responsible for the difficulties we experience.

The antidote to turmoil and hostility is allowing the same peace that characterized the life of Christ to permeate your life. Jesus experienced the inner peace that comes from obedience because of His trust in the goodness and wisdom of His Father's plan: "My food is to do the will of Him who sent Me, and to accomplish His work" (John 4:34).

The Lord's refusal to lash out against His tormentors was the result of His trust in God's justice and power over His enemies: "While being reviled, He did not revile in return; while suffering, He uttered no threats, but kept entrusting Himself to Him who judges righteously" (1 Peter 2:23).

Rule in Your Hearts

God wants you to allow His peace to "rule in your hearts." The word *rule* is an athletic term that means "to umpire." Whenever conflicts arise in your life—whether within yourself or between you and other people—you have a decision to make. You can respond with fear or anger, or you can allow the peace of Christ to have the final say in your life.

I'm reminded of the story about a late-night bull session that occurred at an umpires' convention. Some of the participants were gathered in a room arguing about how they made their calls. "I call them the way I see them," one said. A second umpire said, "I call them the way they are." The third umpire, shaking his head, said, "They ain't nothin' until I call them."

Life's circumstances are like that. We can't always control the events that are thrown at us. We can't even eliminate the internal temptations that entice us. But both temptations and adversities are really nothing until we "call them." Paul therefore urged us to allow the peace of Christ to have the final say in our lives, a peace that can only come from choosing to completely trust in God's love, God's power, and God's wisdom.

Trusting God

What are the benefits of trusting in God's love, power, and wisdom? I can think of at least three ways that trusting God provides freedom in our lives. Let's examine each one of these.

God's Love: Freedom from Past Sins

I recently finished reading a detailed biography of Walt Disney. Contrary to the image many people have of "Uncle Walt," he wasn't the warm, nurturing grandfather that he and his staff worked so hard to portray to the public. Many who worked for Disney described him as a tyrant. On more than one occasion, he fired his entire staff for no reason at all—only to rehire them several weeks later. Why? He felt that living in constant dread of dismissal would motivate his employees to do better work.

On another occasion, Disney summarily fired a long-time employee without any legitimate cause. Years later the employee's wife wrote Disney asking if he'd donate one hundred dollars for a serious eye operation to save her husband's eyesight, which had been damaged by his years of tedious work on animation projects at the Disney studio. The multimillionaire Disney, still unwilling to forgive his employee for some minor offense, responded that he couldn't afford to help.

Fear might work to motivate employees to work harder, but Christians who always question their status before God will never experience intimacy with Him. God takes no delight in having us cower in fear, wondering if we're "in" or "out." He wants us to enjoy the same kind of unity with Him that Jesus Christ experienced:

> Just as the Father has loved Me, I have also loved you; abide in My
> love. (John 15:9)

Are you confident of God's love for you? Do you ever fear that God will dredge up some past mistake and use it as a reason to get even with you? Are you absolutely confident that God will welcome you into His presence when you die?

The key to abiding or resting in God's love is trust—trusting that Christ's death on the cross for you resulted in God's complete forgiveness of your sins. Paul linked the concepts of faith and inner peace (freedom from turmoil) this way:

> Therefore, having been justified by faith, we have peace with God
> through our Lord Jesus Christ. (Romans 5:1)

We can only experience peace with God when we're confident that we've been justified—a legal term meaning "to declare not guilty." This concept is key to the mechanics of God's forgiveness. Our faith—regardless of how much or how little we possess—can't save us. As Paul wrote elsewhere, it's "*by grace* you have been saved *through faith*" (Ephesians 2:8).

Christ's willingness to bear the condemnation from God that we deserve results in our forgiveness. Faith simply connects us sinners to God's forgiveness. Perhaps the following illustration will help.

Suppose I say to one of my daughters, "You can't go out Friday night until the dishwasher is emptied." However, an after-school dental appointment, a last-minute errand, and a phone call from an out-of-town friend consume all of her time, and she doesn't complete her chore. So I end up emptying the dishwasher myself. Seven o'clock rolls around, her friends are out front honking, and when she runs into the kitchen, she realizes what she hasn't done. "Dad, I'm so sorry."

Because she expressed remorse for her actions, I allow her to go out with her friends. Although I'm the one who emptied the dishwasher, I allowed her apology to count for the work I'd performed on her behalf.

Similarly, when we express genuine sorrow for our sin and believe that Christ died on our behalf, our "faith is [counted] as righteousness" (Romans 4:5). The assurance that the barrier between God and us has been removed forever is the basis for our peace from past failures.

God's Power: Freedom from Present Circumstances

What's the biggest concern in your life right now? A spouse whose love has grown cold? A child living in rebellion against you and God? A financial need closing in on you? An illness that your doctors say can't be cured?

Now, I want you to slowly and carefully answer this question: is God capable of changing your situation if He desires? If your answer is yes, then you must conclude that He has some purpose in allowing you to experience your present circumstances. If He has the power to alter your situation, you can rest assured that He's in complete control of your situation.

The gospel writer Luke used an incident from Jesus's life to contrast two distinct responses to storms that blow into our lives:

Now it came about on one of those days, that [Jesus] and His disciples got into a boat, and He said to them, "Let us go over to the other side of the lake." And they launched out. But as they were sailing along He fell asleep; and a fierce gale of wind descended upon the lake, and they began to be swamped and to be in danger. (Luke 8:22–23)

The lake Luke referred to was known as the Lake of Gennesaret or, as we know it, the Sea of Galilee. I've had the opportunity to sail across this lake in a boat similar to the kind Jesus and His disciples used. This body of water is only thirteen miles long and eight miles wide. However, cool air descending from the surrounding mountains collides with the warm air trapped above the lake, producing sudden and violent storms. In Matthew's account of the story, the storm was so fierce that the boat began to shake and water poured in over the sides. Whenever I read this account, I think about the scene in the movie *The Perfect Storm* where that tiny vessel reels against a dark, angry mountain of water.

And what was Jesus doing during this life-threatening storm? While the disciples were panicking, Jesus was snoring.

And they came to Him and woke Him up, saying, "Master, Master, we are perishing!" (verse 24)

Now Luke doesn't come right out and say this, but I have to believe that the disciples must have been a little disgusted with Jesus. How could He sleep so soundly when they needed Him so badly?

I imagine they began to shake the Lord until He awakened. "Jesus, don't You care about what's happening to us?" they asked. "Even if You're fulfilling some sick kind of death wish, at least save us!"

Jesus's response? He wiped the sleep from His eyes, looked around to assess the situation, and said (according to Mark's account), "Hush, be still."

And the wind died down and it became perfectly calm. (Mark 4:39)

Then Jesus looked at His disciples and said, "You ruined a perfectly good nap for this?" Well, not exactly. But He did ask, "Where is your faith?" (Luke 8:25).

Faith? Faith in what?

Jesus's question is the key to understanding the story. Remember Jesus's statement at the beginning of this episode?

Let us go over to the other side of the lake. (verse 22)

With these words, Jesus implicitly assured His disciples that they *would* reach the shore. Their full-blown panic attack resulted from a lack of faith in Jesus's power to keep His promise and fulfill His plan. They really didn't understand who Jesus was.

Who then is this, that He commands even the winds and the water, and they obey Him? (verse 25)

Jesus was aware of the storm, because, as God, He'd created the storm. The roiling water and raging wind were designed as a test to see if the disciples understood Jesus's identity as the Son of God. Unfortunately, they scored an F (which, by the way, doesn't stand for "Faith").

Before you shake your head in disapproval over the disciples' poor performance, ask yourself how you're reacting to the storm you're experiencing right now. Are you panicking? "Lord, where are You? Don't You care about what's happening to me?" Or are you at peace because you understand that no circumstance that arises in your life takes God by surprise? Consider what the late preacher Alan Redpath wrote:

> There is nothing, no circumstance, no trouble, no testing that can ever touch me until, first of all, it has come past God and past Christ, right through to me. If it has come that far, it has come with a great purpose.[1]

Every storm that comes into your life is designed by God for a great purpose—specifically, for the strengthening of your faith. But we need to understand that Satan desires to use the very same storm to destroy your life. Do you remember what Jesus said to Peter before Peter denied the Lord?

> Simon, Simon, behold, Satan has demanded permission to sift you like wheat; but I have prayed for you, that your faith may not fail; and you, when once you have turned again, strengthen your brothers. (Luke 22:31–32)

Jesus knew the storm that was approaching in Peter's life. Jesus knew that, within the next few hours, Peter would be tempted on three different occasions to repudiate the Lord. Satan wanted to use this experience to drive Peter away from Christ forever. But Jesus prayed that this very same test would ultimately strengthen Peter's faith—which it did. Although Peter initially failed the test, his failure allowed him to experience Christ's undeserved forgiveness—an experience that transformed Peter into the mighty leader of the apostles. Satan tempts us to destroy us, but God tests us through the same circumstances in order to strengthen us.

The late psychiatrist and author Scott Peck wrote, "It is in this whole process of meeting and solving problems that life has its meaning.... It is only because of problems that we grow mentally and spiritually.... It is for this reason that wise people learn not to dread but actually to welcome problems and actually to welcome the pain of problems."[2] Peck echoed the words of the New Testament writer James, who encouraged us to

Consider it all joy, my brethren, when you encounter various trials, knowing that the testing of your faith produces endurance. And let endurance have its perfect result, that you may be perfect and complete, lacking in nothing. (1:2–4)

With every storm also comes this promise: just as He delivered the disciples, God will safely deliver us through the storm to the other side. God doesn't always promise to deliver us from the storm, but He promises to lead us through the storm.

I was recently talking with a friend who is facing a massive reorganization in his company. He doesn't know whether he'll have a job in a few months, much less what kind of income he'll earn, just as he's about to send two kids to college. He said, "I don't mind being in this dark tunnel of uncertainty if I just knew there was a light at the end. If God would tell me, 'As you go through the tunnel, you're going to have to fight five monsters, but there's light at the end,' then I think I could go through it."

Amazingly, God *has* made just such a promise. Read carefully these words of assurance the Lord spoke to the prophet Isaiah:

When you pass through the waters, I will be with you;
And through the rivers they will not overflow you.

When you walk through the fire, you will not be scorched,
Nor will the flame burn you. (Isaiah 43:2)

God promises to be with you *through* the chemotherapy, *through* the months of unemployment, *through* the loneliness of a broken relationship, *through* the periods of doubt and depression, and *through* the loss of a loved one. And, just as He did for the apostles, He'll make sure you safely reach the other side.

What guarantee do I have that He will deliver me through the storm to the other side? Consider the promise of Hebrews 6:19–20:

This hope we have as an anchor of the soul, a hope both sure and steadfast and one which enters within the veil, where Jesus has entered as a forerunner for us.

We usually associate an anchor with a large piece of iron dropped into the water to prevent a ship from drifting. But in the first century, an anchor actually helped a vessel arrive safely at its destination.

Many of the harbors in the Mediterranean Sea were laced with dangerous rocks that could easily destroy a tiny ship caught in a storm or carried along by an unexpected gust of wind. But in every harbor, a large rock known as an anchor was firmly embedded in the water close to the shoreline.

When a ship was ready to come into the harbor, the forerunner got into a smaller vessel and took the ship's line with him. He tied it to the large rock or anchor. The ship, now tied to the anchor, could safely be pulled ashore.

The writer of Hebrews employed that imagery here when he taught that Jesus Christ is both your Forerunner and your Anchor. Jesus has already gone before you and passed into heaven; He's made it to the other side. And no matter how uncertain, how turbulent, or how precarious your life becomes, you're tied to Him. He carefully guides you through any circumstances that might shipwreck your life, and He assures your safe arrival on the other side.

God's Wisdom: Freedom from Worry

As I type these words, I face what could be a monumental change in my life. What happens within the next few months will profoundly impact my ministry and my family. I can easily allow a flood of what-ifs to seize control of my thoughts.

Strangely, a year or so from now, when this manuscript is released as a book, the situation will be resolved, and I'll read these words in type. If the past is any indication of the future, I'll probably smile and say to myself, "You worried about nothing. If you'd known then what you know now, you'd have slept much more soundly."

I wish I could punch the Fast Forward button—just for an instant— to see what's ahead. But such a mechanism is not only unavailable, it's also unnecessary for experiencing freedom from worry. Even though I can't see what awaits me, God can see it. And He encourages me to trust in His wisdom and in His goodness.

"For I know the plans that I have for you," declares the LORD, "plans for welfare and not for calamity to give you a future and a hope." (Jeremiah 29:11)

God knows what lies ahead of you, because He has planned what lies ahead of you. His future plans for you are good, not evil. He asks you to simply relax and trust Him.

Author Henri Nouwen wrote about the special relationship that exists between the flyer and the catcher in a trapeze troupe. A moment comes in the performance when the flyer, swinging high above the crowd, must let go of the trapeze. In that instant, the flyer is suspended in midair. He can't reach back for the trapeze, and it's too early to reach for the catcher. Instead, he must wait.

> The flyer must never [try to] catch the catcher. He must wait in
> absolute trust. The catcher will catch him. But he must wait. His
> job isn't to flail about in anxiety. In fact, if he does, it could kill him.
> His job is to be still. To wait. And to wait is the hardest work of all.[3]

When your life hangs in the balance, waiting and being still about your future seem impossible…until you know the Catcher. The Lord encourages us, "Be still, and know that I am God" (Psalm 46:10, KJV).

God's love, demonstrated by His forgiveness of your sins, means He never wants you to fall.

God's power means He's capable of keeping you from falling.

God's wisdom means He sees what's before you and will be there at precisely the right time to prevent you from falling.

You really can trust Him.

A Content Heart

Finding More in Less

Question: "Who's happier? A man with $11 million or a man with eleven children?"

Answer: "A man with eleven children."

Why?

"Because he doesn't want more."

More. It's *more* than a four-letter word. The desire for more is like a thief that robs us of the enjoyment of the present moment. It can destroy relationships, cause anxious thoughts about the future, and make us feel inadequate. It's a cruel taskmaster that won't allow us to rest.

I was reminded again of the destructive power of the desire for more when I read about a church that dismissed its pastor for financial impropriety. An audit revealed that the pastor had incurred thousands of dollars of personal charges on the church credit card, even though the pastor earned several hundred thousand dollars a year.

What would cause a minister—who was already being paid more than most people could ever hope of earning—to risk ending his career, ruining his reputation, and severely damaging the congregation he was serving? The desire for *more*.

More is a disease that is no respecter of persons. Everyone is susceptible to the virus. Sometimes we use other words to describe the same infection of the heart:

- I wish a drove *a newer* car.
- If only I had a *different* mate.
- I'd love to live in a *larger* home.
- I'd do anything for a *better* job.

More. Newer. Different. Larger. Better. They're all symptoms of a dissatisfaction that prevents us from enjoying the present. Please understand, I'm not labeling all dissatisfaction with present circumstances wrong. After all, Orville and Wilbur's discontent with limiting travel to land and sea led to the invention of the airplane. Thomas Edison's dissatisfaction with reading by candlelight led to the invention of the light bulb. Nehemiah's dissatisfaction with the condition of Jerusalem led to the rebuilding of the wall. The apostle Paul's dissatisfaction with the spiritual condition of the Corinthian church led him to write two scathing letters of rebuke that Christians still study today.

The desire for more—or better, larger, different—harms us when it keeps us from enjoying in the present what God has already given us and when it provokes us to worry about the future. Our inability to enjoy today and our anxiety about tomorrow rob us of the benefits of living within the kingdom of God in the present.

Think about it. When Christ finally establishes His visible rule over all of the earth, do you believe His followers will obsess over their 401(k) accounts, lose sleep over their Visa balances, or be envious of those believers who reside in larger mansions? Of course not! We'll experience the total satisfaction that comes from living under God's rule and allowing Him to meet our needs.

But we don't have to postpone that satisfaction to some future eschatological age. God wants us to be free *in this life* from the tyranny of chasing after more, better, different, and larger. The opposite of *more* isn't *less*. Instead, it's *contentment*.

Contentment Is Possible

The word *contentment* comes from a word that means "containment." It describes people who are self-contained, who derive their sense of well-being from their inner resources rather than from their external circumstances. Content people don't tie their happiness to

- the ups and downs of the stock market
- the balance in their retirement account
- their teenager's SAT scores
- the model of automobile they're driving
- their rank on the company's organizational chart

People who have developed content hearts realize that no amount of money, no achievement, no circumstance can quench the insatiable human desire for more. Instead, content people look to inward resources to experience satisfaction.

The life of Jesus Christ reveals that contentment really is possible. Consider Jesus's external circumstances. He had no financial cushion—or, for that matter, any other kind of cushion—on which to rest:

The foxes have holes, and the birds of the air have nests; but the Son of Man has nowhere to lay His head. (Matthew 8:20)

Jesus was constantly dogged (or, had He ministered today, it would be "blogged") by His critics. His family members rejected Him, and His closest associates abandoned Him. His adversaries tried several times to kill Him until they finally succeeded. Yet, in spite of all this, Jesus's life was filled with joy—a joy that He prayed His followers would also experience:

> But now I come to Thee; and these things I speak in the world, that
> they may have My joy made full in themselves. (John 17:13)

Although Jesus illustrated that contentment is possible in this life, the apostle Paul reminded us that contentment doesn't come naturally. When Paul wrote his letter to the church at Philippi, he had plenty of reasons to be discontent with his circumstances. He was in prison, waiting for the verdict in his trial—a verdict that could result in the death penalty. False teachers had invaded the churches Paul had established, and some were using his imprisonment as an opportunity to slander his reputation. In spite of these outward circumstances, Paul encouraged his readers to "rejoice in the Lord always" (4:4).

How did Paul divorce his inward sense of well-being from his outward circumstances? Nothing in Paul's writings suggests that he possessed an overly positive personality. Read his letters carefully and you'd never describe Paul as a born optimist. He had to work at developing a content heart. Contentment is a learned behavior.

> For I have *learned* to be content in whatever circumstances I am.
> (verse 11)

Let me say this again. Contentment doesn't come naturally. In fact, discontentment is part of the basic DNA we inherited from Adam and Eve.

Although they were surrounded by countless trees in the garden, trees that were bearing a variety of delicious fruit, their fixation on what they *didn't* have led to their downfall. "Eat from *that* tree and you'll be truly satisfied," the Deceiver promised.

Sometimes the bait Satan dangles in front of us to satisfy our discontent is inherently sinful (sexual immorality, dishonest financial gain, substance abuse). But I believe that every temptation we consider can be traced to our basic lack of contentment with God's provisions. We think—or Satan whispers—"Since God has not provided you with what you really need to be happy, you'd better start looking out for yourself. Why not try this?" As someone observed, at the root of all sin is contempt for God.

At other times, though, our lack of contentment doesn't result in sin, but in unrest. Author Harold Kushner tells of a rabbi who asked a member of his congregation, "Why is it that you're always in a hurry? You always seem to be running."

He replied, "I'm running after success, I'm running after fulfillment, I'm running after the reward for all my hard work."

The rabbi responded, "That's a good answer if you assume that all those blessings are somewhere ahead of you, trying to elude you and if you run fast enough, you may catch up with them. But isn't it possible that those blessings are behind you, that they are looking for you, and the more you run, the harder you make it for them to find you?"[1]

I recently found a list of goals I had written down more than twenty years ago:

"Pastor church of _____ in attendance." Done.

"Author of _____ books." Done.

"Net worth of $_____." Done.

"Two children." Done.

"National radio and television ministry." Done.

Two emotions hit me simultaneously when I put down the list. I felt profound gratitude to God for allowing me to fulfill these dreams. I also felt genuine amazement over the fact that those completed goals hadn't provided me with any more fulfillment than they had. Why not? Because I'm human and I can't help but focus on those who have achieved more than I have.

Although our church is larger than 99 percent of the churches in my denomination, I can't help but think about those several dozen churches that are larger. And why don't my books do as well as Lucado's or Yancey's? I felt good about my financial situation until I found out about a pastor who makes twice what I earn. And unless I change my name to Swindoll, Myers, or Dobson, I'm a peon in the world of religious broadcasting. So I keep chasing after more.

Don't look at me that way! You know exactly what I'm talking about. Perhaps you, too, are in the relentless pursuit for more, different, newer, or larger. And you're exhausted! Every goal you check off the list only makes you crave more. Writer Patrick Morley shared this parable:

Every morning in Africa when the sun comes up, a gazelle awakens and knows that it must run faster than the fastest lion, or it will perish. Every morning in Africa when the sun comes up, a lion awakens and knows that it must run faster than the slowest gazelle, or it will go hungry. It doesn't make any difference if you are a gazelle or a lion. Every morning in Africa when the sun comes up, you had better be running.[2]

Instead of running, wouldn't you rather be resting? Jesus promised, "Come to Me, all who are weary and heavy-laden, and I will give you rest" (Matthew 11:28). Too many Christians read Jesus's invitation and think,

That's a sweet thought. Someday, when I get to heaven, I'll get all the rest I need. But I don't have time to think about it now.

But Jesus never said you needed to wait until you die to rest. Stop chasing after the money, the title, the relationship, the dream you think will satisfy you. It *won't.* Learn the secret of contentment.

The Benefits of a Content Heart

At the core of a content heart is the conviction that God has already provided us with everything we need to be satisfied in life. That persuasion results in at least three tangible benefits.

Enjoying Where We Are

I love our annual family vacation. Every year Amy and I take our two daughters to the most beautiful place in the world to us: Hawaii. We would sacrifice food and furniture to make our annual trek to the islands. I begin anticipating our July trip sometime in early February. When I exercise in the morning, when I sit through a particularly taxing deacons' meeting, or when I drive the car, I mentally transport myself to the white beaches of Maui. *In just ____ months I'll be there.*

But no sooner do we touch down at the Kahalui airport than I begin thinking, *I only have ____ days left of this vacation.* I begin the countdown until the final few days when I start thinking about *next* year. *In ____ months I'll get to return.*

All of us suffer from a type of "destination sickness." We believe that when we finally arrive at a certain place in our lives, we'll be truly happy. I call it the When-Then Syndrome: "Someday when…, then I'll be satisfied." Jesus Christ didn't suffer from such a disease.

As the Lord knelt in Gethsemane, anticipating the grueling ordeal immediately ahead of Him, He could have thought, *Someday, when I'm seated at the right hand of the Father, then I'll have joy.* But instead He prayed that His followers—who were not facing crucifixion—could experience the same joy He had at that very moment.

As Paul sat in a prison cell awaiting the verdict in his trial, he could have reasoned, *When I find out if I'm going to live or die, then I'll be able to rejoice in the Lord.* But instead he wrote, "But even if I am being poured out as a drink offering upon the sacrifice and service of your faith, I rejoice and share my joy with you all" (Philippians 2:17).

Jesus and Paul refused to postpone until some future time their enjoyment of the lives God had created for them. They successfully battled "destination sickness" by learning the secret of contentment.

Appreciating Rather Than Resenting

I recently had the opportunity to spend some time with megachurch pastor Bill Hybels. He has built one of the largest churches in America, lectured at Harvard Business School, authored numerous best-selling books, and has a ministry being replicated around the globe. Yet in spite of his success, he made a startling admission. "When you reach my age and stage in ministry, you realize that there are certain dreams you had for yourself that just aren't going to happen. And once you come to grips with that, you can enjoy what God has given you."

Throughout the day, some in our group peppered Hybels with questions about other pastors and ministry styles. He never criticized other leaders who had larger ministries, even though some of them would have made easy targets. I left the meeting with the feeling that Bill Hybels is comfortable in his own skin. He's at peace with himself, and that puts him at peace with others.

The New Testament writer James asked the question, "What is the source of quarrels and conflicts among you?" (4:1). Before we look at his answer, how would you answer that question?

- What is the root cause of conflicts between people?
- What motivates a husband to abandon his mate of twenty-five years?
- What sparks most church splits?
- What causes someone to instigate a lawsuit against a one-time friend?

At the heart of most conflicts is not a difference in communication styles, a theological disagreement, or a sincere quest for justice. So what is the source? James said this:

Is not the source your pleasures that wage war in your members?
You lust and do not have; so you commit murder. And you are
envious and cannot obtain; so you fight and quarrel. (verses 1–2)

James wrote that a lack of contentment is the basis for most of our relational conflicts. That dissatisfaction manifests itself in several destructive behaviors. For example, sometimes our discontent leads to extreme acts of aggression against other people. When we delude ourselves into thinking that some possession, some relationship, or some circumstance will fill the void of our empty life, we'll go to almost any extreme to obtain what we don't have. We'll steal another person's possession, mate, or even life if necessary.

Maybe you remember the almost unbelievable story of figure skater Tonya Harding. Her ex-husband and two other men attacked Harding's main competitor, Nancy Kerrigan, during the U.S. Figure Skating Championships in 1994. With Kerrigan's injury forcing her to withdraw, Harding won the event. But after an investigation, figure-skating officials concluded that Harding at least knew about the attack before it occurred, and they stripped Harding of her title and banned her for life from participating or coaching in sanctioned events.

How do you explain rational people who commit irrational acts like adultery, larceny, murder—or even whacking a competitor on the knee? They're provoked into such extreme behavior, James explained, by that craving ("lust") for what they don't have. And that craving is fueled by discontent: "If only I can have _____, then I'll finally be satisfied."

Other times our discontentment manifests itself in a seething envy of another person. This jealousy over what someone else possesses might not lead to outward acts of violence like murder, but we can use other ways to kill a person. For example, character assassination is a favorite indoor sport among Christians, including Christian leaders. When the spotlight shines brightly on some pastor, author, or Christian speaker, you can be sure that a whispering campaign against him or her is already in the works.

"Have you heard about her marriage?"

"His theology needs to be examined more closely."

"I hear his closest associates have some stories to tell."

Occasionally such criticisms are legitimate. However, most times they're rooted in the green-eyed monster called envy—craving what someone else possesses.

Such jealousy isn't limited to Christian leaders. Think about someone you regularly criticize. What's the *real* reason you're willing to destroy that person's reputation? What does he or she have that you desire? If you possessed what you're craving, would you be as critical of that person?

Being at peace with the circumstances of our life is the only way to be at peace with others.

Enhancing God's Reputation

Imagine that a teacher overhears your child talking to a friend at school, complaining about conditions at home: "Our home is filthy with rats running everywhere. My parents leave me home alone so they can party all night. I go to bed hungry every night, because we don't have enough to eat." The concerned teacher immediately contacts child protective services to investigate this obvious case of neglect.

However, when the CPS representative arrives at your home, she's surprised to find an immaculate house with no rodents in sight, a refrigerator and pantry stocked with food, and parents who give every sign of being attentive caregivers. She then relates to you what the teacher overheard your child saying to a friend. How embarrassed would you be? What would you say to your child once the CPS representative left?

I imagine that God is similarly embarrassed when He hears us complaining about our living conditions to anyone who will listen. Children of God who are continually dissatisfied with their circumstances or are anxious about whether they'll have what they need to survive reflect poorly on their heavenly Father. After all, what unbeliever wants to entrust his or her life— or, for that matter, his or her eternity—to a God who can't provide life's basic needs to His own children? That's why Jesus encouraged His followers:

> Do not be anxious then, saying, "What shall we eat?" or "What
> shall we drink?" or "With what shall we clothe ourselves?" For all
> these things the Gentiles eagerly seek; for your heavenly Father
> knows that you need all these things. (Matthew 6:31–32)

Unbelievers ("Gentiles") have every reason to worry about their material needs. A job loss, bankruptcy, or unexpected illness could leave them destitute. But we Christians have a heavenly Father who promises to watch over us and provide for us. After all, Jesus reasoned, if God feeds the birds of the air and if He clothes the lilies of field (see verses 26–30), can't He be trusted to care for His own offspring?

If you're a Christian, you're a living advertisement for God. People read you as they would a billboard. They watch you like they do a television commercial. And they're deciding: "Do I want some of what she has or not?"

Their answer largely depends on your level of contentment. You might claim that your relationship with Christ is a source of great fulfillment. But if you constantly pursue more (or better, larger, or different), will anyone really believe your faith satisfies? If you constantly complain about your income, your job, or your family, will a non-Christian really believe you when you claim, "God loves you and has a *wonderful* plan for your life"?

Becoming like Jesus Christ involves embracing Jesus's life purpose: to glorify God. Jesus Himself declared:

> I glorified Thee on the earth, having accomplished the work which
> Thou hast given Me to do. (John 17:4)

To glorify God simply means to make God look good to other people. Contentment—satisfaction with what we have and faith for what we don't yet have—is a primary way we enhance rather than diminish God's image. As John Piper wrote, "God is most glorified in us when we are most satisfied in Him."[3]

Learning Contentment

Contentment doesn't naturally spring forth from our hearts. Everything around us—as well as within us—wars against being satisfied with what

God provides and instead chooses to be obsessed with what He hasn't chosen to give us. That's why Paul said he had to learn the secret of contentment. As one who struggles with this issue of contentment daily (if not hourly), let me share some practical ways that I've tried to develop a content heart.

Regularly Express Gratitude to God

Light and darkness can't coexist. When you turn on a lamp or open the blinds, light displaces the darkness. In the same way, discontent and gratitude can't exist in the same heart. If you're genuinely grateful for what God has already given you, you can't be discontent over what God hasn't yet provided. The gratitude will displace your discontentment.

Remember the story of the ten lepers Jesus healed? The fact that only one of the ten came back to Jesus to say, "Thank you," illustrates that gratitude isn't an automatic response to God's gifts. We have to work at it.

Expressing thanksgiving to God is more than a ritual before digging into a meal. We must discipline ourselves to take time to genuinely tell God how much we appreciate what He's already given us before we rush into His presence asking for more.

Isn't that what you want from your children? When my daughters start to complain that they don't have the latest model iPod or that their friends are driving newer cars, I never think, *Oh, I better give them what they want so they'll like me.* Instead, my heart and my wallet close. My first instinct is to do less for them, not more.

However, the opposite is also true. The other day I took my older daughter to buy her textbooks for college. When we finished, she got in the car and said, "Dad, I want to thank you for paying for college for me. I have friends who have to work full-time jobs to cover their expenses, and it means a lot that you are doing this for me." At that moment, she could have asked me for just about anything and I'd have given it to her.

The primary benefit of gratitude is its power to quench the insatiable desire for more. Mark Buchanan illustrated the power of gratitude as he told of an experience at a worship service in Africa. Although everyone else was enthusiastically participating in the service, Mark admitted this:

I was too sour to join in. The music sounded squawky. I was miffed at someone on our missions team. I found the food bland, tasteless. I was feeling deprived and misunderstood. I found the joy of others hollow.... I was miserable, and I wanted to wallow in it.

The pastor asked if anyone had anything to share....

"Oh, brothers and sisters, I love Jesus so much," [a woman] said.

"Tell us, sister! Tell us!" the Ugandans shouted back.

"Oh, I love Him so much, I don't know where to begin. He is so good to me. Where do I begin to tell you how good He is to me?"

"Begin there, sister! Begin right there!"

"Oh," she said, "He's so good. I praise Him all the time for how good He is. For three months, I prayed to Him for shoes. And look!" And with that the woman cocked up her leg so that we could see one foot. One very ordinary shoe covered it. "He gave me shoes."

The Ugandans went wild. They clapped, they cheered, they whistled, they yelled.

But not me. I was devastated. I sat there broken and grieving. In an instant, God snapped me out of my self-pity and plunged me into repentance. In all my life, I had not once prayed for shoes. It never even crossed my mind. And in all my life, I had not even once thanked God for the many, many shoes I had.

Thanklessness becomes its own prison.[4]

Gratitude is the key that frees you from the prison of thanklessness and discontent. So I suggest that right now you close your eyes for a moment and thank God from the depths of your heart for what He has given you. Your family. Your job. Your health. Your lack of concern over where you'll sleep tonight and where your next meal will come from.

And I suggest that you make a commitment to never again go to God asking for something more, different, better, newer, or larger without first thanking Him for something He's already done for you.

Recognize the Oasis Illusion

You've seen it in the movies. A man, parched with thirst, shuffles through an endless stretch of white desert sand as the sun relentlessly beats down upon him. He keeps going because he sees an oasis just beyond the sand dune. If only he can make it there, then he'll find the relief he desperately seeks. But when he arrives at the spot, he discovers the palm trees and the spring of clear, cool water were only a mirage. Profoundly disappointed, he doesn't know what to do except keep trudging through the desert looking for the satisfaction that continues to elude him.

All of us have created our own imaginary oasis. We might not readily admit it, but it exists in our mind. Remember the When-Then Syndrome? Our oasis might include a new (or better or different) relationship, coveted recognition, a desired promotion, or a certain sum of money. But we'll never experience contentment until we realize that our personal oasis is only a mirage. Writer Robert J. Hastings imaginatively illustrates this truth, employing a different metaphor in his essay "The Station":

> Tucked away in our subconscious is a vision, an idyllic vision, in
> which we see ourselves on a long journey that spans an entire

continent. We're traveling by train and, from the windows, we drink in the passing scenes of cars on nearby highways, of children waving at crossings, of cattle grazing in distant pastures....

But uppermost in our minds is our final destination—for at a certain hour and on a given day, our train will finally pull into the station with bells ringing, flags waving, and bands playing. And once that day comes, so many wonderful dreams will come. So restlessly, we pace the aisles and count the miles, peering ahead, waiting, waiting, waiting for the station.[5]

"When we reach the station, that will be it!" we cry. "When I'm eighteen." "When I buy a new Mercedes-Benz 450SL!" "When I put the last kid through college." "When I've paid off the mortgage!" "When I get a promotion." "When I reach the age of retirement, I shall live happily after that!"

Sooner or later we must realize there is no station, no place to arrive at once and for all. The true joy in life is the trip. The station is only a dream, and it constantly outdistances us.

Adopt a Purpose Bigger than Yourself

The apostle Paul hadn't always enjoyed contentment. At one time in his life, he was obsessed with obtaining advanced educational degrees and climbing the hierarchy of the Pharisees. But his face-to-face confrontation with Jesus Christ changed the focus and purpose of his life.

Whatever things were gain to me, those things I have counted as loss for the sake of Christ. More than that, I count all things to be loss in view of the surpassing value of knowing Christ Jesus my Lord, for

whom I have suffered the loss of all things, and count them but
rubbish in order that I may gain Christ. (Philippians 3:7-8)

When I read these words, I picture a man who is dying of thirst on a
raft in the middle of the ocean. Out of desperation, he starts drinking the
salty ocean water. But it only increases his thirst and, ultimately, leads to his
death.

Earlier in his life, Paul had tried to satisfy his own inner desire for significance by chasing after more and more achievements. Instead of quench-
ing his thirst, however, those successes only caused him to crave more.

Once Paul discovered the satisfaction that comes from a relationship
with Jesus Christ, however, the apostle's perspective on external circumstances changed dramatically. Now he knew the secret of being "self-
contained," and that allowed him to view negative situations in a different
light. As Paul sat in prison facing what could have been the end of his life,
he wrote this:

> Now I want you to know, brethren, that my circumstances have
> turned out for the greater progress of the gospel, so that my im-
> prisonment in the cause of Christ has become well-known through-
> out the whole praetorian guard and to everyone else, and that most
> of the brethren, trusting in the Lord because of my imprisonment,
> have far more courage to speak the word of God without fear.
> (1:12–14)

If Paul's life purpose had been peace and prosperity, then being imprisoned would have been a catastrophe for him. But Paul had adopted a purpose in life larger than his own personal comfort. He was obsessed with

sharing the gospel of Christ with as many people as possible, and that goal served as a lens through which he viewed "negative" circumstances. So, far from being a setback, Paul's imprisonment actually worked to help him fulfill his life's objective. How?

First, Paul was chained to a different Roman guard every six hours, every day, for more than two years. What do you think Paul talked about with those soldiers during those hours? The weather? The stock market? The outcome of the latest chariot races? Maybe. But a significant part of those conversations included Paul sharing the gospel with so many of these guards that Christianity spread like wildfire throughout this elite unit of the emperor's army. Additionally, as a result of Paul's boldness, other Christians were encouraged to share their faith. Most people would consider imprisonment a tragedy. Paul viewed it as a triumph because he had a larger purpose in life.

Paul's words remind me of a conversation I had with Ed Scearce, director of the Steve Wingfield Evangelistic Association. Ed has made many trips to Romania. He told me of a pastor who, before the fall of communism, was arrested for sharing the gospel and sentenced to work as an exterminator—the lowest job imaginable in Romania. Yet, far from being distraught over his sentence, the pastor was elated. Why? As he went from house to house killing rats, he realized that he had a wonderful opportunity to spread the gospel throughout the country!

So let me ask you: What's *your* real purpose in life? What are you really chasing after? Your answer will determine how you view what appear to be negative circumstances. Someone has written:

If for me to live is money, then to die is to leave it all behind.

If for me to live is fame, then to die is to quickly be forgotten.

If for me to live is power and influence, then to die is to lose both.
If for me to live is possessions, then to die is to depart with nothing
      in my hands.
But if for me to live is Christ, then to die is gain.

Such a conclusion can only come from someone who has learned the secret of developing a content heart.

A Serving Heart

Discovering the Key to Greatness

Epitaphs attempt to reduce someone's life to a sentence or two on a slab of stone. Recently I ran across some epitaphs that may or may not be legitimate:

HERE LIES LESTER MORE; FOUR SLUGS FROM A .44—NO LES, NO MORE.

SIR JOHN STRANGE; HERE LIES AN HONEST LAWYER, AND THAT IS STRANGE.

HERE LIES THE BODY OF JONATHAN BLAKE; STEPPED ON THE GAS INSTEAD OF THE BRAKE.

I TOLD YOU I WAS SICK.

The late talk-show host Johnny Carson was once asked what he'd like on his tombstone. "More to come," he replied, referring to the graphic that would appear between commercials on his program. Mel Blanc, the voice of many of the famous Warner Brothers cartoon characters such as Bugs Bunny and Daffy Duck, chose one of his character's signature lines for his tombstone: "That's all, folks!"

What about you? If you were to choose a sentence to characterize your life on earth, what would it be? How would you most like to be remembered? Would you cite some accomplishment of which you're particularly proud? How about a personality trait that friends and family find appealing? Would you be tempted to take this one last chance to settle a score or correct a misconception about you

Thinking about your grave marker might be a little depressing, so let's change our focus for a moment. Suppose you were asked to create an epitaph for the empty tomb of Jesus Christ. What phrase would best capture the essence of His life?

"King of kings, Lord of lords"?

"The Alpha and Omega"?

"All things have been created by Him and for Him"?

Each of those phrases expresses the majesty of the second Person of the Godhead, but each of them was written by someone other than Jesus. I suspect that if Jesus Himself composed His own epitaph, He'd probably choose the one He used to describe Himself in Mark 10:45:

For even the Son of Man did not come to be served, but to serve, and to give His life a ransom for many.

When you stop and carefully consider the above words, they almost take your breath away. Think about this: no one deserves to be served more than the eternal Son of God, the King of kings, the Creator of all things. In ages past, before Jesus entered the world via Bethlehem, He was worshiped by the heavenly beings (see John 17:5). In the future, all believers will bow before His throne saying, "Worthy is the Lamb that was slain to receive power and riches and wisdom and might and honor and glory and blessing" (Revelation 5:12).

But at the core of Christ's heart is a desire to serve us rather than be served by us. In fact, in the above passage, John said that the reason we'll worship Christ is because of His willingness to serve us by meeting our greatest need—the forgiveness of our sins (see verse 9).

We shouldn't be surprised then by the high value that Jesus placed upon our learning to serve other people. Consider just a few of Jesus's teachings concerning servanthood:

You know that the rulers of the Gentiles lord it over them, and their great men exercise authority over them. It is not so among you, but whoever wishes to become great among you shall be your servant, and whoever wishes to be first among you shall be your slave. (Matthew 20:25–27)

But the greatest among you shall be your servant. And whoever exalts himself shall be humbled; and whoever humbles himself shall be exalted. (Matthew 23:11–12)

Then the righteous will answer Him, saying, "Lord, when did we see You hungry, and feed You, or thirsty, and give You drink?"… And the King will answer and say to them, "Truly I say to you, to the extent that you did it to one of these brothers of Mine, even the least of them, you did it to Me." (Matthew 25:37, 40)

If God really desires for us to become like His Son, then we'll never be more like Jesus than when we serve others. But how do we develop a serving heart?

What Is Servanthood?

To serve someone means to meet that person's needs. Whether the most pressing need is a loaf of bread, a cup of water, or an article of clothing, a servant does everything in his power to provide it, regardless of the sacrifice required. At the essence of servanthood is placing another person's interests above your own.

But let's be honest. Few of the people we associate with are dying for a loaf of bread, a drink of water, or a coat to keep them warm in the winter. Still, our friends or family members do have very real needs that we're capable of meeting. The bottom-line question we grapple with, however, is whether we're willing to place their needs above our own needs. I faced that dilemma recently.

One of the networks that carries our television programs e-mailed me last night about a content issue regarding next week's program and requested that we make a change. The staff member in charge of that ministry was on a well-deserved vacation with his family. However, I knew that he needed to be aware of the situation, so I called him on his cell phone to apprise him of the problem. "Dr. Jeffress, I'm driving right now and wondered if you could call my assistant and give her the information so she can take care of it?"

I wish I could tell you that I responded, "Of course. Don't worry about it and enjoy the time with your family." I didn't. In fact, I'm embarrassed to tell you my response and how I formulated it. Instantly, I thought to myself, *I don't work for you; you work for me. I'm the teacher on a nationally broadcast ministry, and I shouldn't lower myself to take care of mundane details like this.*

I didn't voice those sentiments, but I acted upon them. "No, you call your assistant and relay the information" was, I'm ashamed to say, my curt reply.

My staff member's greatest need was to spend time with his family. Although I had it within my power to meet that need, I chose to place my need to free myself from details and to maintain my place above his on the organizational chart.

Every day you face the same dilemma: will you place someone else's needs above your own? If you're a husband, will you place your wife's need for conversation after dinner above your need to unwind and watch television? If you're a parent, will you place your child's need for a quality education above your need for early retirement? If you're a wife, will you place your husband's need for admiration above your need to correct him?

Face it. Serving others isn't natural or easy. From the time we draw our first breath, we're programmed to think in terms of me, my, and mine. What baby do you know would ever say or even think, "Mom, I know you're tired from staying up all night, so you can feed me after you get some rest"?

Selfishness—placing our needs above others' needs—isn't something we naturally outgrow. Some churches today, for example, remain war zones as young adults and senior adults battle for their preferred worship style: "This is *my* church, and we're going to worship *my* way!"

Since getting older doesn't guarantee that we'll get better, how do we develop a serving heart? Jesus Christ provides us with both an illustration and an understanding of the ingredients of genuine servanthood.

Servanthood: An Illustration

I recently saw a television commercial advertising a video that golfers can purchase to improve their swing. By calling the toll-free number and giving the operator access to your credit card, you receive the instructional tape and watch an expert hit a golf ball. Presumably, by watching a professional repeatedly, you can emulate his actions and enjoy his success.

Instead of improving our swing, however, the apostle Paul encouraged us to improve our serve by carefully considering and then imitating the actions of the all-time serving Pro, Jesus Christ. Before examining this greatest illustration of servanthood in history, let's look at the context of Paul's words recorded in Philippians 2.

The church at Philippi had become its own war zone. Doctrinal problems and relational conflicts were ripping the congregation apart. Out of deep concern over these divisions in the church he'd founded, Paul placed his finger on the real source of the conflicts: me, my, and mine. Selfishness. Paul's solution?

> Do nothing from selfishness or empty conceit, but with humility of mind let each of you regard one another as more important than himself; do not merely look out for your own personal interests, but also for the interests of others. (2:3–4)

Think of others as more important than yourself. Place the interests of others above your own. In other words, develop a servant's heart. "Nice thought, Paul. But exactly how do you pull that off?" Paul, a master teacher himself, understood the importance of using illustrations when instructing. So, instead of giving the Philippians an 800 number to call to order a videotape, he provided them with the supreme example of servanthood to study and imitate:

> Have this attitude in yourselves which was also in Christ Jesus…
> (verse 5)

Paul followed this simple admonition with a detailed description of Christ's example of servanthood:

> …who, although He existed in the form of God, did not regard equality with God a thing to be grasped, but emptied Himself, taking the form of a bond-servant, and being made in the likeness of men. And being found in appearance as a man, He humbled Himself by becoming obedient to the point of death, even death on a cross. (verses 6–8)

I hesitate to clinically dissect this paragraph, which commentator F. B. Meyer described as standing in "inapproachable and unexampled majesty." But beyond the beautiful poetry and the instructive description of the work and life of Christ found in this passage, we also discover three essential ingredients for developing a servant's heart.

The Humble Heart

I had a seminary professor who described what he called "the glorification of the worm" ceremony. A pastor stands at the back of the sanctuary after the service and demonstrates his humility as congregants file by offering an obligatory compliment. In mild protest, the pastor responds, "I am nothing." Yet neither party is persuaded that the pastor means what he says.

True humility involves an honest assessment of both our strengths and our weaknesses. In Romans 12, before launching into a detailed explanation of spiritual gifts, Paul encouraged each of us

> Not to think more highly of himself than he ought to think; but to think so as to have sound judgment, as God has allotted to each a measure of faith. (verse 3)

Despite this admonition, some Christians view themselves as God's gift to the church. "You don't know how lucky you are to have me—and don't you forget it" is their attitude. But Paul said that just as no part of the human body can survive without a connection to the rest of the body, no Christian is self-sufficient. We need one another.

An equally destructive attitude, however, is the belief that we are lowly worms who have nothing valuable to contribute. In truth, every Christian has been empowered with a unique spiritual gift that is vital to the success of the church. You need other Christians—and other Christians need you.

True humility acknowledges our gifts but attributes them to the Giver of those gifts. You never find Jesus making any "I am a worm" statements. He had a clear understanding of who He was. "I and the Father are one," He claimed (John 10:30). When He was arrested in the garden, Jesus reminded Peter that His death was voluntary, not required:

> Or do you think that I cannot appeal to My Father, and He will at once put at My disposal more than twelve legions of angels? (Matthew 26:53)

Honestly, that statement sounds a little boastful, don't you think? It almost sounds like the rich kid who, about to be beaten up by the schoolyard bully, says, "You better watch out, because you don't know who my daddy is." *Almost*—until you realize that Jesus could have received that angelic assistance if He'd simply requested it. Instead, He voluntarily surrendered what was rightfully His to serve a greater purpose. It's impossible to surrender something you don't have. For example:

- I can't give up my Lexus to aid the poor…because I don't drive a Lexus.
- I can't sell my eight-thousand-square-foot home and donate the proceeds to missionaries, because I don't own an eight-thousand-square-foot home.
- I can't allow a wounded soldier to take my first-class airplane ticket while I sit in coach, because my church doesn't pay for me to fly first class.

Before I can surrender a privilege, I must first possess it—and realize that I possess it. Paul reminded us that Jesus Christ—the personification of humility—was fully aware that He was equal to God the Father:

…who, although He existed in the form of God, did not regard equality with God a thing to be grasped. (Philippians 2:6)

The Sacrificial Heart

In spite of His heavenly position, Jesus Christ humbly demonstrated the second vital characteristic of a servant: sacrifice.

A few years ago I was in a meeting of pastors during which Rick Warren, pastor of Saddleback Church and author of the megaseller *The Purpose-Driven Life,* addressed our group. Next to the Bible, his book is the best-selling nonfiction book of all time. He regularly appears on national television programs, has been invited to the White House to counsel the president, and personally disciples some of the most influential people in the business and entertainment world.

Still, Warren is one of the humblest people I've ever known. That evening he told our group, "God gives us affluence or influence for one reason: to build His kingdom, not ours." Warren lives by that conviction, residing in the same modest home he's lived in for years and giving away 90 percent of his income. Rick Warren has dedicated his money, his influence, and his time to meeting the genuine need to know Jesus Christ that people around the globe have.

I've defined *servanthood* as "meeting the needs of other people." But doing this requires giving up what we value, such as money, time, or influence. If we can grasp the idea that anything of value in life has been given to us by God, sacrificing a position or a possession becomes a *little* easier.

Again, consider the example of Jesus. Although He enjoyed all the privileges and perks of being equal to God the Father,

> He did not regard equality with God a thing to be grasped, but
> emptied Himself, taking the form of a bond-servant, and being
> made in the likeness of men. And being found in appearance as a
> man, He humbled Himself by becoming obedient to the point of
> death, even death on a cross. (Philippians 2:6–8)

We need to clearly understand what Jesus emptied Himself of. First of all, Jesus couldn't surrender being God anymore than I can give up being five feet nine inches tall. Deity was the essence of Jesus's very being. Instead, Jesus surrendered the privileges that went along with being equal to God. Gifted writer Dorothy Sayers described what that surrender entailed:

For whatever reason God chose to make man as he is—limited and suffering and subject to sorrows and death—He had the honesty and the courage to take His own medicine. Whatever game He is playing with His creation, He has kept His own rules and played fair. He can exact nothing from man that He has not exacted from Himself. He has Himself gone through the whole of human experience, from the trivial irritations of family life and the cramping restrictions of hard work and lack of money to the worst horrors of pain and humiliation, defeat, despair, and death. When He was a man, He played the man. He was born in poverty and died in disgrace and thought it well worthwhile.[1]

Why was Jesus willing to sacrifice His comfort, reputation, and rights? Because He cared more about satisfying your needs than His own. He placed your interests above His.

Quite honestly, serving others rarely requires the kind of severe sacrifice Jesus made. Few of us will ever face the dilemma of surrendering our physical life for someone else. But sacrifices don't have to be drastic to be costly. Sometimes servanthood requires us to surrender our pride (as I illustrated—negatively—with my co-worker). Other times, placing someone else's needs above ours requires us to sacrifice other things of value.

For the past year, our older daughter has gone to college in our community. Although she moved out of our home and into a house a mile away from us, we enjoy seeing her just about every day when she drops by. And we've also enjoyed the modest tuition payments of a state school.

However, our daughter is now convinced that God wants her to attend a Christian university about four hours away from us. When I saw the tuition costs, my first thought was, *I don't want to buy the school; I just want my daughter to attend.* The church I serve recently gave me a nice raise, for which I made all kind of plans. Forget that! We're devoting all of it—and much more—to the cause of higher education. But we do so happily, knowing that we're helping our daughter realize God's plan for her life.

Sometimes serving others means surrendering our time. If you've ever read a time-management book, you've learned the importance of ignoring distractions such as telephone calls or urgent requests from others so you can concentrate on your to-do list. As practical as such advice may be, it goes against Jesus's call to us to serve others.

Think about the numerous interruptions Jesus endured in His ministry in order to serve others, including a woman who was bleeding uncontrollably, a co-worker's mother-in-law who had become ill, and a paralytic who dropped in (or, more accurately, dropped down) in the middle of one of Jesus's sermons. Contradicting one of the most basic tenets of modern management, Jesus made Himself a servant to the tyranny of the urgent, placing the needs of others above His need to complete His day's to-do list.

Recently, I've been reading the diaries of President Ronald Reagan. Perhaps no president in modern history accomplished more than he did. The end of the Cold War, the rebuilding of the nation's military, and the longest economic expansion in history are just some of the late president's extraordinary successes. Still, stories abound about his willingness to make a phone call, write a letter, or intervene on behalf of people who had nothing to offer in return.

One of the most frequently told stories by Reagan's biographers concerned an eighty-three-year-old woman named Frances Green. Frances had little money but faithfully mailed in one dollar a year to the Republican National Committee. One day Frances received a beautiful invitation to come to the White House and meet President Reagan. She failed to notice that the RSVP card also suggested a large donation to ensure face time with the president. Not realizing that she was part of a bulk mailing, she believed the president wanted to see her because of her dollar-a-year support.

Frances spent her limited funds on a train ticket for the four-day journey from San Francisco to Washington DC. When she arrived at the White House gate, the guard informed her that her name wasn't on the list and she couldn't go in. An executive with the Ford Motor Company was behind her and, realizing something was wrong, asked Frances to relate her story. The executive told Frances to come back the next morning at nine and meet him at the gate.

Once inside the White House, the executive informed a presidential aide about Frances Green's situation. The aide arranged for Frances to receive a tour of the White House and a brief introduction to Reagan the next day.

The following morning Frances arrived at the gate to meet her president. The day was marked by frantic activity. The attorney general had just resigned, and an international crisis demanded President Reagan's full attention. The Ford Motor Company executive gave Frances a tour of the White House and then took her to the Oval Office, hoping she might catch a glimpse of Reagan on her way out. High-level generals were coming in and out of the Oval Office as Frances arrived. President Reagan, glancing out the open door, saw Frances. With a warm smile, he waved her into the office.

"Frances! Those darn computers, they fouled up again! Had I known you were coming, I would have come out there to get you myself." He invited her to sit down to talk about their home state of California, their families, and their life experiences.

That day, the most powerful man in the world sacrificed time he really didn't have to meet the need of someone who could never do anything for him. Why? Because Ronald Reagan understood that his position and power had been given to him for one purpose: to serve others.

The Faithful Heart

Frankly, we'll never consistently place other people's interests above our own without the faith that God will one day reward us for doing so. We'll never trade privilege for sacrifice until we're convinced we'll experience a payoff in our future.

You might wince at that observation. You want to think that we should be willing to serve others without any promise of future reward. You might believe that serving others for future gain is unseemly, if not downright unspiritual. But before you draw that conclusion, consider both the example and the instruction of the greatest Servant of all time. The writer of Hebrews revealed Jesus's motivation for enduring the agony of the cross:

Jesus,… who *for the joy set before Him* endured the cross, despising the shame, and has sat down at the right hand of the throne of God. (12:2)

Some Christians unintentionally romanticize the Cross by singing sentimental songs or wearing religious jewelry that masks the true horror of death by crucifixion. Jesus didn't willingly endure the pain of Calvary because He was some type of spiritual sadomasochist who relished the pain of those hours. The above scripture indicates that Jesus endured the suffering of the cross for one reason: by faith, Jesus believed that God would reward Him for His sacrifice.

God never asks us to divorce the concepts of service and reward. He never requires us to make sacrifices for the sheer pleasure—or pain—of surrendering something important to us. In fact, God has designed us in such a way that we won't consistently place His interests or the interests of others above our own without the assurance that one day we'll profit by doing so.

> And without faith it is impossible to please Him, for he who comes
> to God must believe that He is, and that He is a *rewarder* of those
> who seek Him. (11:6)

Like the writer of Hebrews, Paul also connected Jesus's humiliation on the cross with His future exaltation before the entire universe:

> He humbled Himself by becoming obedient to the point of death,
> even death on a cross. Therefore also God highly exalted Him, and
> bestowed on Him the name which is above every name, that at the
> name of Jesus every knee should bow, of those who are in heaven,
> and on earth, and under the earth, and that every tongue should
> confess that Jesus Christ is Lord, to the glory of God the Father.
> (Philippians 2:8–11)

Serving God and others might mean temporarily setting aside our need for recognition and reward, but God never asks us to permanently surrender our desire for either. Jesus never said, "Whoever wishes to be great among you is a self-serving jerk who doesn't have a clue about true Christianity." Instead, Jesus legitimized our basic need for significance by providing the pathway for achieving genuine greatness:

> Whoever wishes to become great among you shall be your servant;
> and whoever wishes to be first among you shall be slave of all.
> (Mark 10:43–44)

Occasionally, life provides us with a glimpse of the future rewards of servanthood. The weekend following September 11, 2001, syndicated columnist Peggy Noonan went to lower Manhattan to witness the relief work taking place at Ground Zero. She watched the endless procession of trucks leaving the site, trucks filled with teams of construction workers, police, firefighters, and medical technicians. Noonan described it as a procession of the not-so-rich and famous.

But as they rolled past the assembled group of onlookers, these ordinary workers were treated as celebrities. Noonan joined the crowd as they shouted out, "God bless you!" and "We love you!" Noonan wrote:

> I looked around me at all of us who were cheering. And saw who they were. Investment bankers! Orthodontists! Magazine editors! In my group, a lawyer, a columnist and a writer. We had been the kings and queens of the city, respected professionals in a city that respects its professional class. And this night we were nobody. We were so useless, all we could do was applaud the somebodies, the workers who, unlike us, had not been applauded much in their lives.[2]

What Peggy Noonan witnessed that day was a small preview of coming attractions in heaven. One day, Jesus promised, those who have served others will experience the unending applause of heaven's residents and the eternal approval of God.

Steps to Developing a Servant's Heart

Some years ago I was seated in an office and noticed on a table a beautifully bound leather book with this title stamped on gold letters: "My Humility…and How I Achieved It." Naturally, curiosity led me to open the book, and I discovered it was filled with blank pages! The joke underscored a basic truth. Anyone who thinks he or she has achieved humility still has a long way to go.

The same principle applies in developing a servant's heart. We'll never arrive at the place where we can say, "*Now* I am a servant."

We'll always struggle to acknowledge that every good thing in life comes from God.

We'll always find it painful to surrender what we believe is ours for the benefit of someone else.

We'll always wonder if our temporary sacrifices will result in eternal gain.

Still, like each of the other qualities God desires in our life, we can take some positive steps toward developing a servant's heart. Even though placing the interests of God or others above our own interests will always be somewhat difficult, it can become more of a reflexive response.

In this chapter's closing paragraphs, I want to review the three essential components of a servant's heart and suggest some practical action steps for developing such a heart.

Practice Humility

We began this chapter talking about epitaphs. Take a moment and write down a paragraph describing the accomplishments for which you'd most like to be remembered. Then ask yourself the same question Paul asked the Corinthian Christians:

> What do you have that you did not receive? But if you did receive it,
> why do you boast as if you had not received it? (1 Corinthians 4:7)

What possession, position, or accomplishment in your life isn't directly or ultimately attributable to what God or others have done for you? There is nothing wrong with honestly acknowledging the abilities, accomplishments, possessions, or positions of honor that are yours. The key is to attribute those gifts to the Giver of all good gifts.

I encourage you to stop right now and thank God for those gifts. And then, as we discussed earlier, make it a habit to begin your prayer time not with requests for more, but with thanksgiving for what God has already done for you.

Live as a Sacrifice

Realizing that every good thing in our life is a gift makes it easier to surrender our possessions for someone else's benefit. But letting go takes practice, especially given our natural tendency to hold on tightly to the things we value most.

Here's a challenge I encourage you to accept: determine that at least once a day for the next thirty days you're going to surrender something of value for someone else. For example, your time might be your most valuable commodity. So, instead of checking off items on your to-do list or watching a television program, you might sacrifice thirty minutes to listen to someone who really needs to talk, to call someone who needs to hear from you, or to visit someone in the hospital.

Maybe your sacrifice will involve giving up money you've designated for something you wanted so that you can meet the need or even the want of another person. Just as Jesus emptied Himself of His divine rights, we must regularly empty ourselves of the things we value most.

Focus on Faith

If you keep a spiritual journal, your answers to the question I'm about to ask might be an interesting list to begin now and to add to through the years. If not, at least give the question some thought occasionally. Here it is: "What sacrifices have I made in this life that I expect God to reward me for in the next life?"

As we saw earlier, without the promise of reward, we won't consistently sacrifice our time, our rights, or our material possessions. Even for Jesus, the "joy set before Him" provided the motivation for the agony of the cross.

Just as there is no sacrifice without reward, there will be no reward without sacrifice. What are you sacrificing in your life right now that is worthy of a future reward? I'm thinking of things beyond our normal responsibilities such as loving our mates, caring for our children, and obeying God's commands.

Jesus voluntarily surrendered His rights as God not because He was obligated to do so, but because He was a servant at heart.

Are you?

A Praying Heart

Communicating with the One Who Loves You Most

I want you to pray in every situation and not be discouraged," Jesus commanded His disciples.

"Pray without ceasing," Paul instructed the Thessalonian church (1 Thessalonians 5:17).

Easier said than done for most of us. Yes, I'm aware of the surveys in national newsmagazines claiming that the general population has a great interest in prayer. More Americans will pray this week than will exercise or have sex. Nine out ten Americans pray "regularly." We're told that 75 percent of Americans pray every day.[1]

But, given people's natural tendency to place themselves in a favorable light, I'm skeptical of these polls. If people actually attended church as frequently as they report they do, most congregations would be in perpetual building programs. If people donated as much money as they claim to, most congregations would be declaring dividends every year. Similarly, I suspect that if we actually prayed as often as we say we do, our world—not to mention our own lives—would be in much better shape.

Scratch beneath the surface of these surveys and I imagine what you'll find is that most of our "prayer time" is limited to an occasional outburst of "Help me, Lord." Not that anything is wrong with that kind of prayer. The apostle Peter found that request to be quite effective as he began to sink in the churning Sea of Galilee. Yet limiting our communication with God to 911 calls for divine assistance doesn't result in a satisfying experience for either God or us.

Let's move from the theoretical to the personal. Why don't you pray more? I realize that, by asking such a question, I'm making an assumption. But my pastoral experience tells me it's probably an accurate one. More than likely, the following are true for you:

- You feel guilty about your prayerlessness.
- It takes a titanic struggle to spend even five or ten minutes a day talking to God.
- When your will does win out over your desires and you begin to pray, you find it very difficult to concentrate.
- Deep down you really wonder if beyond the momentary relief you feel, prayer really makes any difference.

Talking to an invisible God, who rarely seems to answer immediately or audibly, is hard work. You might be encouraged to know that the apostle Paul struggled with prayer. In fact, Paul pleaded with the Christians in Rome to "strive together with me in your prayers" (15:30). The word translated "strive" is *agonizomai* from which we derive our word *agonize*. This word originally described the struggle of a wrestler in an athletic contest. Any way you look at it, prayer is hard work.

Jesus Himself found prayer unsatisfying at times. During the horrendous experience of the Cross, He cried out, "My God, my God, why have you forsaken me?" (Matthew 27:46, NIV). Yet the heavens remained silent, and Christ felt abandoned at the most critical moment of His earthly life.

Why is prayer so difficult for so many of us? Many times we excuse our prayerlessness by saying that we lack the time. But Oswald Chambers placed that excuse in its proper perspective: "Remember, no one has time to pray; we have to take time from other things that are valuable in order to understand how necessary prayer is."[2] The real reason we can't find time to pray is because we aren't convinced of the value of prayer.

I read about three pastors discussing the various postures of prayer while a telephone repairman worked on the phone system. One minister said that he found folding his hands helpful. Another minister commented that bowing in humility before God was crucial. The third minister said that he prayed while flat on his face before God. The telephone repairman couldn't remain quiet any longer. "I have found the most powerful prayer I ever prayed was [while I was] upside down, hanging by my heels from a power pole, forty feet above the ground."[3]

Perhaps we find it difficult to schedule time to pray because we lack those hanging-upside-down experiences. Most of the time, our lives appear to be right side up. We feel self-sufficient, capable of solving our dilemmas without any need for divine intervention. Why take time away from activities that produce tangible results to devote time to prayer, since its effectiveness seems uncertain at best?

Some people also allow theological questions to discourage them from praying. The most frequent question I'm asked as a pastor is, "If God is sovereign and is going to do what He wants, why should I bother to pray?" This question isn't original. The philosopher Immanuel Kant believed it "an absurd and presumptuous delusion" to believe that prayer could in any way alter God's predetermined plan. In Kant's defense, God Himself declared, "I the LORD do not change" (Malachi 3:6, NIV). Yet the very same

God also said, "My heart is changed within me; all my compassion is aroused" (Hosea 11:8, NIV).[4]

One of the most vivid examples of the connection between our prayers and God's activity is found in the book of Revelation. Before the beginning of the trumpet judgments during the Great Tribulation, a silence in heaven lasts for thirty minutes. During this interval, an angel collects all the prayers offered by believers on earth who have cried out to God for His judgment against evildoers.

When the angel offers these prayers before the throne of God, the prayers are suddenly hurled to the earth, followed by "peals of thunder and sounds and flashes of lightning and an earthquake. And the seven angels who had the seven trumpets prepared themselves to sound them" (8:5–6).

Author Walter Wink observed, "The message is clear.... History belongs to the intercessors, who believe the future into being."[5] Or, as Andrew Murray wrote, "Prayer is the power by which that comes to pass which otherwise would not take place."[6]

Jesus on Prayer

All my questions surrounding the relationship between my prayers and God's sovereignty melt away when I examine the life of Jesus Christ. The Son of God viewed regular conversations with God as essential to His spiritual survival. Prayer was the foundation of Jesus's life and ministry.

Think about it. Jesus was God in human flesh, yet He felt the need to pray. He was perfect, conceived by the Holy Spirit, yet He prayed. He possessed the power to perform every imaginable miracle, including raising people from the dead, yet He prayed.

Mark 1 records one of the busiest single days of Jesus's ministry—as jam-packed as an entire season of *24*. Jesus spent the entire day preaching, casting out demons, and healing the sick. An exhausting day of ministering to His sheep kept the Lord from needing to count sheep to fall asleep that night. But most remarkable to me is what happened the next morning:

> And in the early morning, while it was still dark, He arose and went
> out and departed to a lonely place, and was praying there. (verse 35)

One Sunday, Bobby Bowden, head football coach at Florida State University, spoke at our church. Coach Bowden, a committed Christian who uses his public influence to spread the message of Christ, shared with our congregation that the key to maintaining his spiritual health is arising every morning at 4:00 a.m. to pray and read his Bible. "Of course, I go to bed at 7:00 p.m. every night!" Bowden added.

Not the Lord. Mark's gospel records that the day before, "when evening had come, after the sun had set, they began bringing to Him all who were ill and those who were demon-possessed" (verse 32). In other words, Jesus probably didn't finish ministering to the people until late into the previous night.

When the alarm sounded the next day at 4:00 a.m., Jesus had every reason to hit the Snooze button and roll over. After all, He'd been busily engaged in ministry the day before. Why not sleep in?

Don't forget that Jesus was fully human as well as fully divine. That means He experienced the same physical limitations we experience, including hunger, thirst, sore throats, and exhaustion. On this particular morning, every muscle in His fatigued body probably pleaded with Him to stay in bed just a little longer. Given all that Jesus had done the day before, surely His heavenly Father would forgive Him for skipping one daily quiet time.

But for Jesus, spending time conversing with His Father wasn't optional. It was actually essential to His spiritual survival. As Martin Luther would say hundreds of years later, "To be a Christian without prayer is no more possible than to be alive without breathing." As you search through the gospels, you find Jesus praying during pivotal moments in His life: His baptism, His temptation in the wilderness, prior to the calling of the apostles, before major miracles, the moments before His betrayal in Gethsemane, and during His crucifixion.

But Jesus didn't limit His praying just to major events. Instead, conversing with God was part of the natural rhythm of His life on earth, and it continues to be part of His existence in heaven. The author of Hebrews wrote that Jesus "always lives to make intercession for [us]" (Hebrews 7:25). Have you ever wondered what Jesus spends His time in heaven doing? At this very moment He's praying for you—asking God to forgive you, to direct you, and to protect you.

A Word to Us

Jesus encouraged us to pray not only by His own example but by His exhortations. Perhaps one of His simplest-to-understand but most-difficult-to-apply teachings about prayer is found in Luke 18. The Lord had just predicted the suffering that will occur prior to His return to earth. Against that backdrop, Luke reported this:

> Now He was telling them a parable to show that at all times they ought to pray and not to lose heart. (verse 1)

I don't know about you, but I'm more likely to pray when an answer from God seems probable rather than impossible. I keep a prayer list where I record my requests and God's answers. Recently, I've added several difficult issues with which I'm struggling. The solutions to these complex problems will require the supernatural intervention of God. But instead of making those issues the focus of my prayers, I avoid them. I spend my time asking God for important but ultimately immeasurable requests. (How do I know when He has "blessed my wife," "blessed my family," or "blessed my church"?) I finally figured out that I'm prone to pray those "safe" prayers so that I'm not disappointed by what seems to be God's unwillingness or inability to solve the thorny issues in my life.

When my world starts caving in and God's help seems like just a remote possibility, I tend to panic and grab the reins myself. When my lifeboat has sprung a leak and is taking on water, bailing seems more practical than praying! But Jesus says it's exactly at those times that we need to pray and not lose heart. To drive home that truth, Jesus told His disciples a story about a helpless widow and an unrighteous judge.

The widow was being victimized by people (maybe some of those nasty Pharisees) who were taking advantage of the legal system that allowed for frivolous lawsuits. Since the widow had no money to defend herself, she was in danger of losing the few possessions she had.

Without a husband to protect her, and unable to afford an attorney, all the woman could do was plead with the judge for assistance. Unfortunately, the judge prided himself as someone who didn't fear God or "respect man" (verse 2). By advertising his lack of a moral compass, he was signaling to the widow's adversaries that he could be bought off. He might as well have placed a sign around his neck reading, "BRIBES ARE WELCOME HERE!"

Still, the widow continually begged the judge for protection. At first, Jesus said, the judge was unmoved by her pleas. But then came the kind of unexpected twist that occurs in all of Jesus's stories:

And for a while he was unwilling; but afterward he said to himself, "Even though I do not fear God nor respect man, yet because this widow bothers me, I will give her legal protection, lest by continually coming she wear me out." (verses 4–5)

Had Jesus stopped here and said to His listeners, "May God touch your hearts with the truth of this story and enable you to apply it to your lives. Amen," we'd draw the wrong conclusion about prayer. Aware that persistent children keep begging their parents for a new video game until the parents give in, we might assume that prayer involves manipulating God or wearing Him down. Knowing our propensity to draw such a conclusion, the Lord clearly stated the correct application:

Hear what the unrighteous judge said; now shall not God bring
about justice for His elect, who cry to Him day and night, and will
He delay long over them? (verses 6–7)

This isn't a parable of comparison, but of contrast. God isn't like an unrighteous judge who possesses neither ethics nor compassion, and we shouldn't think of ourselves as helpless paupers who have no legal standing before God. The contrast is that if an unrighteous judge can be moved to act on behalf of a stranger, how much more will our righteous and loving God be moved to action by the sincere pleas of His children, whom He loves?

Because of who God is and who we are in relationship to Him, Jesus said we should "pray at all times and not lose heart." That means we shouldn't limit our praying to situations when the answer seems probable; we should definitely also pray when the answers seem impossible.

When the car breaks down in the middle of traffic, pray.

When the notice of the layoff comes, pray.

When that son or daughter persists in rebelling against you and God, pray.

When the tests results from the doctor aren't good, pray.

And when we pray, we can be assured that our loving heavenly Father is listening and will answer us in His time and according to His plan.

Why Pray?

When we parents give a command and our children ask "Why?" our favorite response is often, "Because I told you so." The same answer *should* satisfy the natural question, "Why pray if God is sovereign and He will do whatever He chooses to do anyway?"

Fortunately, Scripture provides a more detailed answer to that question by providing at least four practical benefits for developing a praying heart.

Prayer Develops Our Intimacy with God

The movie *The Good Shepherd* is a fictional account of the beginning of the Central Intelligence Agency. In the story, the lead character, played by Matt Damon, is recruited by the CIA and sent overseas immediately after he gets married. During those years of separation, his wife (played by Angelina Jolie) gives birth to their first child. The parents communicate only sporadically with each other.

One of the most poignant scenes in the movie occurs when Damon's character finally returns home to be reunited with his wife and to meet his now seven-year-old son. After walking through the front door and introducing himself to his boy, he inquires, "Is your mother here?" When she appears, you can feel the awkwardness of this husband and wife who have grown so far apart.

"If you don't mind," she says later, "we'll sleep in separate beds until we get to know each other again." From Damon's expression you get the idea that he minded a lot, but he apparently didn't feel that he could object.

We might think Jolie's character should respond more affectionately to a husband who was away serving his country. But her very natural response reveals an important truth about relationships: intimacy can't be mandated; it must be cultivated. A marriage license, a ceremony, and the exchange of rings aren't sufficient to develop a relationship between a husband and wife. They must spend time together.

Of course, the same is true of our relationship with God. If we want to develop a relationship with Him, we need to spend time with Him. As a pastor, I frequently encounter people who say, "I feel so distant from God. Honestly, I'm not sure I even believe that He exists." When I gently inquire about the time they spend talking with God and reading His Word, the usual response is that it has been months—if not years—since they prayed or read the Bible. And they wonder why they feel distant from God? You can't be intimate with Someone with whom you communicate only sporadically.

For a number of years, I had a close friend with whom I talked about everything in my life. This person knew me as well as just about anyone. However, for no reason other than the passing of years and changes in our individual lives, we began communicating less frequently. Now I might talk with this person once every few months, but the conversations have become superficial. "How are you doing? Seen any good movies or read any good books? How's your family?"

To probe any deeper would seem awkward, because I'm out of the habit of sharing on a deeper level. In fact, I doubt that I'll continue to make the phone calls much longer because they seem so superficial. Our friendship is on life support and will probably expire soon due to a lack of frequent communication.

Prayer—communicating with God—is vital to keeping our relationship with Him alive and vibrant. Without times of intimate and honest sharing with God, our relationship with Him will deteriorate and eventually expire.

If you've flown before, you know that at the beginning of every flight, a flight attendant demonstrates how to use the oxygen masks that will drop down in case the plane loses its pressurization. I've been flying regularly for fifty years and have never once seen those masks deployed, so like most passengers I pay little attention to the announcement. Still, it's nice to know that it's there in case of an emergency.

One writer pointed out that most people treat prayer like a spiritual oxygen mask. We assume we can make it through life without it, but it's nice to know prayer is available in extreme situations. But Jesus taught—through both His words and His example—that prayer is more like oxygen itself. Without it, our relationship with God will die.

Prayer Unleashes the Power of God

Imagine Jesus providing this alternate ending to His parable in Luke 18: "And the unrighteous judge responded, 'Although I have no intention of protecting this widow from her adversaries, her constant pleading has helped develop our relationship.'" Would such a conclusion motivate you to "pray at all times and not lose heart"? Getting to know the judge better wasn't the widow's reason for begging him to act on her behalf. She wanted him to do something!

Let's be realistic about prayer. The primary reason we pray is the hope that our intercession will move God to act on our behalf. If God didn't intend to answer our prayers, would we keep on asking?

Yes, developing intimacy with God is a valuable benefit of prayer, but it's not the primary motivation for prayer. We ask, expecting God to answer. We ask, believing God won't do certain things unless we ask. "You do not have because you do not ask," James wrote (verse 4:2).

Obviously, our asking is no guarantee that God will act. The Bible doesn't provide any blanket guarantees that God will do whatever we ask—even if we ask with all the faith in the world.

Last week my younger daughter pleaded with me to allow her to ride in the car with her boyfriend. "Not until you're twenty-five," I responded. Not really. However, we do have a rule that until she's sixteen, she can't be alone in the car with a boy. I refused to grant her request—and I do so for her own protection. But the realization that I might say no doesn't keep her from asking! Deep down—*way* deep down—she knows I want what is best for her.

The same holds true of us in our relationship with God. Deep down, we know He wants what's best for us. That's why Scripture promises, "And this is the confidence which we have before Him, that, if we ask anything *according to His will,* He hears us" (1 John 5:14). Any promise in the Bible that God will answer our prayers means that His answer will fall within the protective boundaries of His will.

The fact that God's yes answers are limited to those requests within His plan shouldn't limit our desire to pray. Rarely do we know before the fact whether or not something is "according to His will." We ask and then we trust that God will answer in a way that mysteriously fuses together our best interests and His eternal plan.

When our prayers are in alignment with God's plan, the results can be electric. John Piper describes prayer as "the splicing of our limp wire to the lightning bolt of heaven."[7]

Elijah experienced the powerful results of praying according to the will of God. On Mount Carmel, surrounded by the false prophets of Baal, God's prophet sought to demonstrate to them and to all of Israel that Jehovah, not Baal, was the true God. Elijah planned to do this by asking God to miraculously consume a water-soaked burnt offering:

> O LORD, the God of Abraham, Isaac and Israel, today let it be
> known that Thou art God in Israel, and that I am Thy servant,
> and that I have done all these things at Thy word. Answer me,
> O LORD, answer me, that this people may know that Thou,
> O LORD, art God, and that Thou hast turned their heart back
> again. (1 Kings 18:36–37)

Elijah, whose name means "Yahweh is God," had dedicated his life to proving to the world that only one true God exists. Elijah's prayer that day not only fit with his life purpose, but more important, it was according to the will of God. Elijah revealed that this contest between the gods had been God's idea: "I have done all these things at Thy word." So how did God respond to a prayer offered in accordance with His will?

> Then the fire of the LORD fell, and consumed the burnt offering
> and the wood and the stones and the dust, and licked up the water
> that was in the trench. (verse 38)

What caused God to answer Elijah's prayer so dramatically? It wasn't the length of the prayer (only sixty-three words in the English text). And we can't credit God's answer to the frequency of Elijah's prayer. Unlike the prophets of Baal who prayed from morning until evening, Elijah only asked God once. Further, Elijah's prayer lacked the emotional displays that characterized Baal's prophets who "leaped about the altar" (verse 26), cried with a loud voice, and cut themselves.

If the answer to Elijah's prayer can't be traced to length, repetition, or emotion, why did God respond so quickly? Because Elijah tapped into the secret of answered prayer: praying according to the will of God.

When we pray according to God's will, God sometimes responds immediately. At other times, His answer might come later. For more than two years, I've been praying about a relationship my daughter was in that I knew wasn't according to God's will. Frankly, it's been the major concern of my life, and it has often consumed my thoughts. Sometimes I was so overwhelmed with anxiety that I'd try to pray and no words would come. But I knew beyond any doubt that I was praying according to the will of God.

A few weeks ago my daughter came into our kitchen and announced that she had broken off the relationship. Would she have done this if I and others hadn't been praying for her? I can't say for sure. But I know that, in my mind, a connection exists between my request and God's answer—a connection that motivates me to speak to Him about other concerns in my life.

Prayer Protects Us with the Peace of God

On a trip to Greece, a group of us traced the second missionary journey of Paul. Seeing the ruins of Corinth and Ephesus provided us with great insight into Paul's letters to the churches in those cities. When we visited the Areopagus in Athens, I could picture the apostle standing before the great philosophers and delivering his famous sermon "To an unknown god" recorded in Acts 17.

But for me, the most fascinating stop on our tour was Philippi, where the gospel was first preached in Europe. Today, you can still go to the stream where Paul led Lydia, the seller of purple, to faith in Christ. And you can also peer into the inner dungeon—which is nothing more than a large hole—where Paul and Silas were chained after being nearly beaten to death. How did they react to such harsh treatment?

But about midnight Paul and Silas were praying and singing
hymns of praise to God, and the prisoners were listening to them.
(Acts 16:25)

"Listening to them"? I believe that's one of the greatest understate-
ments in the entire Bible! I imagine those prisoners thought Paul and Silas
had been struck in the head one too many times. How could anyone pray
and sing at a time like this?

The stock answer that I've heard—and preached—is that prayer and
praise were the result of Paul's supernatural peace in spite of his circumstances. The apostle's unwavering confidence in God's control over his life
gave him the ability to pray in the direst of circumstances.

But I now realize I've gotten it backward all these years. Prayer wasn't
the result of Paul's freedom from anxiety. Prayer was instead the source of
his peace of mind. How do I know that? Because ten years later Paul wrote
these words in his letter to the Philippian Christians:

Be anxious for nothing, but in everything by prayer and supplica-
tion with thanksgiving let your requests be made known to God.
And the peace of God, which surpasses all comprehension, shall
guard your hearts and your minds in Christ Jesus. (4:6–7)

Paul didn't write these words from the comfort of a pastor's study, but
from the confines of a Roman prison. Once again he faced an uncertain
future as he awaited the verdict in his trial, a verdict that would determine
whether he lived or died.

Have you ever awaited the outcome of a medical test? The twenty-four
or forty-eight hours seem interminable. You can't help but imagine the
worst.

Paul had to wait months to hear the verdict of his trial. Guilty or not guilty? Life or death? How could anyone live with that kind of prolonged uncertainty? Paul's advice to "don't worry about anything, but pray about everything" isn't some sweet, spiritual adage to be engraved on a plaque or embroidered on a pillow. These words represent the secret to Paul's emotional and spiritual survival.

Of course Paul was concerned about the outcome of his trial in Rome, just as he'd been concerned about his life ten years earlier when he was imprisoned in that dungeon in Philippi. Yet in both situations Paul was powerless to do anything to effect his release other than pray.

And it was prayer—an honest pouring forth of his feelings and desires to God—that resulted in an inexplicable peace of mind and heart. And just as that Roman guard to whom Paul was chained stood over him, so God's peace will stand watch over our emotions and thoughts, protecting us from those paralyzing thoughts of "What if . . ."

I once heard Dr. David Jeremiah encourage his congregation to make a "Worry List." Write down everything you're concerned about or even think you might be concerned about. Then, on another sheet of paper, write the words "Prayer List" at the top. Draw a line through each item on your "Worry List" as you transfer that item to your "Prayer List." When you pray about these concerns rather than stew over them, the inexplicable peace of God will engulf you and wash away your concerns.

Prayer Aligns Our Will with God's Will

Speaking to God—and allowing Him to speak to us—isn't just a remedy for worry. It's also a primary means God uses to transform our heart, especially our desires. A. W. Tozer wrote, "The hard work of prayer is getting yourself into a state of mind in which you prefer the will of God over your own." Jesus taught the same truth in the model prayer: "Thy kingdom come. Thy will be done, on earth as it is in heaven" (Matthew 6:10). The Lord instructed us to say this not as a mantra, but as a sincere expression of our heart's desire.

Admittedly, it's not always easy to prefer God's will over our own desires. After all, our primary motivation in prayer is usually to get *our* will done on earth. We hope that repeated entreaties will somehow cause our heavenly Father to see the wisdom of giving us what we want.

But the essence of praying with faith is trusting that however God chooses to answer is best. Praying with faith doesn't mean trying to conjure up some positive feeling that what we want to happen will take place. Instead, praying with faith means being at peace with whatever God chooses to do, because we trust His wisdom and His goodness.

As I've mentioned, right now I'm praying about a specific issue in my life that could greatly impact my ministry, my family, and the entire course of my life. On some days I awaken feeling one way about the issue. On other days, I feel like another outcome would be better. After months of ambivalent feelings, I'm emotionally exhausted and have given up praying either way. Instead, I'm saying, "God, do whatever You want to do. You know best."

When Jesus sweat drops of blood in the Garden of Gethsemane, He didn't hesitate to pour out His feelings about the ordeal He would soon face on Calvary. "Father,…let this cup pass from Me," Jesus cried out (Matthew 26:39). But He quickly followed that plea with another request: "Yet not as I will, but as Thou wilt" (verse 39). Only a comma separated Jesus's first request for deliverance from His ultimate desire for God's will to be done.

I believe that the more frequently we pray, the less time will elapse between our desiring our will and our desiring God's will. The ultimate goal of prayer is getting God's will done on earth rather than getting our will done in heaven.

Developing a Praying Heart

As we close this chapter, I want to leave you with four simple and practical suggestions for how to develop a praying heart.

Don't Complicate Prayer

The KISS principle ("Keep It Simple, Stupid") helps us in just about every area of life, including intercession. Countless seminars, sermon series, and books on prayer leave us with the impression that the subject is so complicated we shouldn't dare to attempt it until we're skilled at it, any more than we'd try to operate a jetliner without having a pilot's license.

We've been led to believe that, to employ another metaphor, prayer is some mysterious code requiring the right words spoken in just the right order—and only then will God's power be unlocked. Nothing could be further from the truth. In fact, Jesus taught just the opposite:

> And when you are praying, do not use meaningless repetition, as the Gentiles do, for they suppose that they will be heard for their many words. (Matthew 6:7)

Think about it. Could God ever be impressed by our choice of words? ("What a beautiful word picture Sally has used today! I'm going to answer her prayer right away!") Does any statement in the Bible suggest that God prefers long prayers over short ones? Jesus Himself certainly didn't think so.

If God isn't looking for an impressive vocabulary or a remarkable word count in our prayers, then what *does* He value? Simplicity and sincerity.

I recently conducted the funeral service for a young mother in our church who left a husband and two little girls behind. I can't begin to describe to you the sadness I felt as I looked at those children during the service and watched them walk behind their mother's casket at the conclusion of the service. As the pallbearers were placing the casket in the hearse, the six year old daughter turned and asked me with hopeful eyes, "Pastor, do you think this Sunday we could sing 'Healing Rain' at church? I really like that song."

She didn't embellish her request with a lot of polysyllabic words. She didn't ask repeatedly. But I answered immediately. "Of course we can, honey." Anything I could do to lessen her pain, I wanted to do. And so with one call on my cell phone to the music minister, her request became a reality. She had a need, and I had the power to meet that need. Why would I have done otherwise?

Richard J. Foster reminds us of the importance of praying simply:

Nothing is more central to the spiritual life than prayer, for prayer ushers us into perpetual communion with the heart of God. And there are many things to learn about this life of constant conversation with the Holy One.

But we must beware of making things too complicated. Like children coming to their parents, so we come to God... We bring our heart cries to a loving Father. Like the mother hen who gathers her chicks under her wings, so our God cares for us, protects us, comforts us....

So no matter how much we study the labyrinthine realities of prayer, let us forever come as children to a loving Abba who delights to give and to forgive.[8]

Use a Pen and Pad (or Computer) for Prayer

The spiritual tradition I grew up in affords the same respect to written prayers as it does to snake handling. We just don't do that. Occasionally, a deacon who is terrified at the thought of speaking in public will be asked to pray in our services. Once the coast is clear and (almost) every eye is closed, the deacon discreetly reaches into his coat pocket and pulls out a sheet of paper from which he reads. The few members who feel it's their duty to keep an eye on everything happening in the service are disgusted. "If he has to read his prayer, why even bother?"

But I've discovered that the greatest benefit of written prayers occurs when composing the prayer rather than the offering of it. The discipline of writing your prayers forces you to be specific in your thoughts and helps prevent the mindless banalities that characterize so many prayers (think "lead, guide, direct" versus "bless me, bless this, bless that").

Even though we might not completely write out the majority of our prayers, keeping a prayer journal of our requests is a good way to encourage specificity in our prayers. Through the years I've kept a running list of my requests on one side of a legal tablet, and on the corresponding side I've noted how God answered each request. Such a record keeps me focused when I speak to God. It jogs my ever-diminishing memory about important items to converse with God about. And it reminds me of answered prayers for which I need to thank Him.

Yes, I realize that conversing with God should involve more than asking. Jesus's model in Matthew 6 teaches us that our prayers should include an expression of our genuine desire for God's glory, a confession of sin, and adoration of His name. But the majority of the model prayer includes requests for specific action by God on our behalf ("give us bread," "forgive our sins," and "deliver us from evil").

In fact, as I look at the greatest prayers in the Bible, including the model prayer in Matthew 6, Jesus's priestly prayer in John 17, or Paul's prayers for the Philippian Christians in Philippians 1, each contains specific requests. I haven't been able to find a prayer anywhere in the Bible where the pray-er was not asking God to do something.

Paul encouraged the Philippians to "tell God your needs and don't forget to thank him for his answers" (4:6, TLB). Keeping a record of your requests to God is an invaluable tool for doing just that.

Begin and End Your Day with Prayer

When I was six years old, my irreverent, cigar-chomping accordion teacher Al Trick taught me a lesson about performing I've never forgotten. A veteran of vaudeville, Mr. Trick said to me one day, "Son, the most important part of performance is your first note and your last note. As long as you get those right, everything else is fluff."

Prayer works a lot like those opening and closing notes: how you start and how you close your day shape all of the moments in between. King David, for instance, understood the importance of beginning each day talking with and listening to God:

In the morning, O LORD, Thou wilt hear my voice;
In the morning I will order my prayer to Thee and eagerly watch.
(Psalm 5:3)

Nothing in this text indicates that David spent hours in prayer in the morning or that he didn't pray at other times during the day. But David understood that how he began his day set the tone for the next twenty-four hours. C. S. Lewis advised this:

It happens the moment you wake up each morning. All your wishes and hopes for the day rush at you like wild animals. And the first job of each morning consists in shoving them all back; in listening to the other voice, taking that other point of view, letting that other larger, stronger, quieter life come flowing in.[9]

Here's a simple suggestion. Before you allow your feet to touch the floor in the morning, take a moment and speak to God about your plans, your concerns, and your desire for His favor during the day. You'll be amazed at how beginning your day by talking with God will increase your desire to continue the conversation throughout the day.

Likewise, before you drift off to sleep at night, take a moment to close your day in prayer. David made an interesting contrast between the nocturnal activities of the unrighteous and the righteous. The ungodly person "plans wickedness upon his bed" (Psalm 36:4). His final thought of the day is, "What can I do tomorrow that is even more evil than what I did today?"

Okay, so that might be a little extreme. Few people probably spend the final waking moments of the day plotting their rebellion against God. Instead, they close their day just as they began their day and spent their day—without any thoughts of God at all.

Listen to David's instruction to those who truly want to please God with their lives:

Tremble, and do not sin.
Meditate in your heart upon your bed, and be still.
Offer the sacrifices of righteousness,
And trust in the LORD. (Psalm 4:4–5)

Without being unnecessarily graphic, let me remind you that David's bed had been the scene of one of his most regrettable failures—his adulterous liaison with Bathsheba. Yet in Psalm 4 David said that his bed could also serve as an altar to God. By spending the final moments of his day looking back over the previous twenty-four hours, confessing his transgressions, expressing his gratitude for God's blessings, and acknowledging his dependence on God's protection through the night hours, David offered "sacrifices of righteousness."

And he encouraged us to do the same.

Redeem Random Moments

If you're like me, your life gets filled with important meetings to attend, key decisions to make, and essential activities to perform. But between those critical events each day are minutes of time that can easily be frittered away as we await the next big thing. I'm referring to time spent driving to an engagement, standing in line at the post office or supermarket, or waiting for the next appointment. Some people always have a book to read or a report to complete on their computer. But most of us simply waste those moments, concluding that there's not enough time to do anything substantial.

Why not use those bits of time to engage in conversation with God? Pray for those you care about. Ask God to give you favor for the next big thing. Confess that you're tired and need His strength. Request God's wisdom regarding a decision you're facing.

You don't even have to wait for a lull in the day's activities to pray. It's possible and very profitable to converse with God even as you perform other tasks. Thomas Kelly wrote:

> There is a way of ordering our mental life on more than one level at once. On one level we may be thinking, discussing, seeing, calculating, meeting all the demands of external affairs. But deep within,

behind the scenes, at a profounder level, we may also be in prayer and adoration, song and worship and a gentle receptiveness to divine breathings.[10]

And that's the secret to developing a praying heart. The more you pray…the more you'll continue to pray.

I read this week about a famous actress in Hollywood who fainted at a red carpet gala event. When asked by reporters later what happened, she responded, "I forgot to breathe." Sounds ridiculous, doesn't it?

No more ridiculous than forgetting to pray.

The Transformed Heart

Creating a Plan to Change Your Life

Nearly a year has elapsed since I first began thinking about clutter-free Christianity and studying the subject of spiritual transformation. Much has happened in my ministry and personal life since I typed the opening words of chapter 1 many months ago. But all of it—both the good and not so good—has convinced me even more of the importance of this topic in my own life and yours.

Perhaps the best way to close this book would be to distill the nearly two hundred pages of information you've read into three concluding insights about spiritual transformation.

Transformation Is Essential

I've just returned from dedicating the new offices of a Christian cardiologist who attends our church. He was reared as a Hindu in India, but he became a Christian and has led many of his family members to Christ. He's one of the boldest witnesses for Christ I've ever known. On many occasions he's told patients facing death, "I'll do everything I can to help you, but first I want to talk with you about the only Person who can help you if you should die." Talk about getting someone's attention!

Both the doctor and I are in the heart business. His primary focus is ensuring that the thirteen-ounce pump inside our chest cavity is functioning properly. When he detects an irregular rhythm or a lack of sufficient blood and oxygen, the doctor prescribes the proper medication, suggests a change of behavior, or even advises a major operation to correct the problem. He understands that as the heart goes, so goes the entire body.

My focus is on the spiritual heart of individuals, because I understand that as the heart goes, so goes the entire person. The heart represents the essence of who we are—our thoughts, our decisions, and our emotions. From this center of our spiritual being flow all of the issues of life, including

- our decision to obey or rebel against God's commands
- our choice to pray about a troubled marriage rather than abandon it
- our ability to be at peace rather than being fearful in the face of an uncertain future
- our willingness to forgive an offender rather than seek revenge
- our satisfaction with our possessions rather than our craving more
- our desire to meet someone else's needs rather than our own

Life is the sum total of the decisions we make, and our every decision is determined by the condition of our heart. As a pastor, I see my job as helping people appreciate the benefits of a healthy heart, enabling them to recognize the symptoms of a diseased heart, and assisting them in developing a plan to ensure the long-term health of their heart.

Once a year my doctor performs his own evaluation of the condition of my heart. Sometimes he'll place me on a treadmill and attach a mass of wires to my chest to make sure my heart operates correctly under extreme circumstances. Other times, he'll order a CAT scan to calculate the buildup of any plaque in my arteries that might restrict the flow of blood.

The closer the date of my physical approaches, the more likely I am to modify my behavior. I'm less likely to skip my exercise and more likely to reduce my caloric intake as I face my day of reckoning. The writer of Hebrews reminded us that God is constantly evaluating the true condition of our spiritual heart:

> And there is no creature hidden from His sight, but all things are
> open and laid bare to the eyes of Him with whom we have to do.
> (Hebrews 4:13)

The word translated "laid bare" refers to a criminal being led to his execution. In biblical days it was common for a prisoner to have a dagger strapped around his neck with the point upward, fixed just below his chin, so that he couldn't bow his head in shame. He was forced to look up so that all could see his face and know of his guilt.

When we die, we'll all face a final judgment of our lives. For Christians, this will be a judgment resulting in rewards, but non-Christians will face a judgment resulting in eternal condemnation. This final evaluation, however, doesn't preclude God from judging our hearts every minute of every day.

Woody Allen's award-winning film *Crimes and Misdemeanors* portrays the story of a wealthy Jewish ophthalmologist, Judah Rosenthal, who grew up in an Orthodox family. His father constantly reminded him, "The eyes of God are always upon you."

Through the years, Judah loosens himself from his spiritual moorings, becomes involved in an adulterous relationship, and finally hires a hit man to murder his mistress, who is threatening to expose the affair. In a dream sequence, a rabbi appears to Judah and asks, "Don't you think God sees?"

Judah replies, "God is a luxury I can't afford."

God isn't a luxury; He's a reality. And the fact that His eyes are always upon us should be a strong motivation to pay attention to the condition of our heart.

Transformation Is Desirable

If you've ever been involved in a Scripture memory program, you've probably committed the second part of John 10:10 to heart. That's where Jesus claimed, "I came that they might have life, and might have it abundantly." I've always wondered why we only quote this portion instead of the entire verse. The first half of the verse provides a stark contrast that emphasizes the power of Jesus to fulfill His promise:

> The thief comes only to steal, and kill, and destroy; I came that they might have life, and might have it abundantly.

Only when you understand the Enemy's diabolical plan for your life can you truly appreciate what Christ offers you. Satan wants to steal your peace of mind and contentment, kill your relationships through unforgiveness, and destroy your faith in God's power and goodness. But Jesus said that you don't have to be a victim of Satan's destructive designs on your life. You can experience certain God-given graces to the point of overflowing:

- peace of mind when your world seems to be spinning out of control

- grace toward others in spite of what they do to you
- satisfaction with what God has generously provided you
- confidence in an uncertain future

And the best news is, you don't have to wait until you die to experience this kind of existence! The practical benefits of a transformed heart can begin right now and extend throughout eternity.

In his essay "Meditation in a Toolshed," C. S. Lewis described the relationship between this life and the next one using the analogy of a beam of light in a dark toolshed. When he entered the dark shed, he noticed the beam of light coming in through the crack at the top of the door. At first, he focused on the floating specks of dust in the band of light: "I was seeing the beam, not seeing things by it." But then he moved, and his view changed.

I saw no toolshed, and (above all) no beam. Instead I saw, framed in the irregular cranny at the top of the door, green leaves moving on the branches of a tree outside and beyond that, 90 odd million miles away, the sun. Looking along the beam, and looking at the beam are very different experiences.[1]

Eternal life is a continuum that begins with the here and now and then reaches forever into the hereafter.

Perhaps another analogy will effectively illustrate the immediate benefits of a transformed heart. A friend of mine is organizing a new bank, and he has invited me to invest in it. Although I probably could quadruple my money when the bank is sold in eight or ten years, until that time no dividends will be paid. That investment is dead money for nearly a decade. On the other hand, I could take that same amount of money and earn 5 percent a year in a money-market account or watch it grow at about 10 percent a year in a stock mutual fund. Should I choose a possible long-term windfall or immediate but moderate dividends?

Many Christians wrongly assume that deciding to live within the kingdom of God—submitting to God's rule over every part of their lives—is an investment that pays no dividends until they die. But as we've seen throughout this book, the payoff of a transformed heart can begin right now and extend throughout eternity.

Transformation Must Be Intentional

As we saw in chapter 3, before our hearts can be transformed, they must first be revived. Only God is capable of bringing to life a spiritual heart that is dead and unresponsive to Him. But once it begins pumping, we're responsible for developing and maintaining a healthy heart. The theological term that describes this process is *sanctification*. The transformation of our heart into one that beats like Jesus's heart requires time, energy, and a plan. It never just happens. Oswald Chambers explained that reality:

> The question of forming habits on the basis of the grace of God is a very vital one. To ignore it is to fall into the snare of the Pharisee— the grace of God is praised, Jesus Christ is praised, the Redemption is praised, but the practical everyday life evades working it out. If we refuse to practise, it is not God's grace that fails when crisis comes, but our own nature. When the crisis comes, we ask God to help us, but He cannot if we have not made our nature our ally. The practising is ours, not God's. God regenerates us and puts us in contact with all His divine resources, but He cannot make us walk according to His will.[2]

Spiritual transformation grows out of a partnership with God. He supplies the grace—the desire and supernatural power to be like Christ—but we must supply the willpower. The apostle Peter began his second letter praising God's grace that has supplied us with "everything pertaining to life and godliness" (1:3). So, are we free to just relax, let go, and let God do all the work of spiritual transformation?

No way, Peter said. Yes, God has provided everything we need, but we also have a responsibility:

> Now for this very reason also, applying all diligence, in your faith
> supply moral excellence, and in your moral excellence, knowledge;
> and in your knowledge, self-control, and in your self-control, perse-
> verance, and in your perseverance, godliness; and in your godliness,
> brotherly kindness, and in your brotherly kindness, Christian love.
> (verses 5–7)

Let me say it again: spiritual transformation is a partnership between God and us. About this cooperative effort, Philip Yancey wrote, "The partnership binds so tight that it becomes hard to distinguish who is doing what, God or the human partner. God has come that close."[3]

Practical Steps to Transform Your Heart

Enough of the theoretical. Let's get intensely practical in these closing pages.

Paul prayed that the believers in Philippi would experience "progress" in their faith (1:25). The word translated "progress" refers to the removal of trees, boulders, and any other obstacles that would impede an advancing army.

How are you progressing in developing a heart like Jesus Christ? Are you removing the barriers that hinder your spiritual growth? Are you making measurable progress in becoming like Him? You might want to consider the following checklist as part of your self-evaluation:

- Do you find it easier to forgive people today than you did five years ago?
- Are you more obedient to Christ's commands than you were a year ago?
- Are you less likely to panic when you receive bad news than you were several years ago?
- Are you more satisfied or less satisfied with your income, possessions, relationships, and accomplishments than you were at this time last year?
- Can you cite two or three examples this past year when you sacrificed something significant for the benefit of another?
- Do you talk with God more regularly or less regularly than you did a year ago?

You and I are either progressing or regressing on the road to becoming more like Jesus Christ. Which is it for you? If you don't have a specific plan for transforming your thoughts, your affections, and your decisions to become more like Christ's, are you really surprised by your lack of progress?

Allow me to suggest a simple plan to help you become more intentional about developing each of the qualities we've discussed in this book.

A Forgiving Heart (Chapter 4)

Ponder these questions:

- What aspect of forgiving others do you find most difficult? Why?

- Can you think of any wrong that would be impossible for you to forgive? Explain.
- What conscious action do you need to take to forgive someone who has wronged you? What practical steps can you take in order to forgive so you can begin enjoying the benefits of God's kingdom now?

Memorize Ephesians 4:31–32.

Take action: After reading Jesus's parable in Matthew 18:21–35, ask God to bring to mind three people you need to forgive. On the basis of the debt from which God has forgiven you, make the decision to release your offenders from their obligation to you.

An Obeying Heart (Chapter 5)

Ponder these questions:

- What's your toughest struggle when it comes to obeying God?
- Over what area of your life do you most try to retain control? How does this prevent you from complete, Christlike obedience to God?
- Which principle for developing an obedient heart do you need to work on most: making obedience a priority, reminding yourself of God's constant presence, obeying all of God's commands, or focusing on the benefits of obedience. List some steps you can take to practice that particular area of obedience.

Memorize 1 John 2:3–5.

Take action: What one thing do you know God wants you to start doing? What one thing does God want you to stop doing? Are you ready to act on the truth God has revealed to you in these two areas?

A Trusting Heart (Chapter 6)

Ponder these questions:

- This chapter included definitions of faith (page 91) and of a trusting heart (page 92). Record these definitions in a journal or in the space below. Then personalize these statements so that trusting God seems more doable to you. Write your own version in your journal or below.

- What area of freedom are you not experiencing because you're not trusting God?

- What storm are you going through now or have you gone through recently? Why can understanding God's promise to make sure you "safely reach the other side" help you carry on each day? List some ways you can remind yourself of the imagery of Christ as both the Forerunner and Anchor who safely guides you.

Memorize Jeremiah 29:11.

Take action: Reflect on several times in your life when God has brought you safely through a storm. Recall how you felt in the middle of the storm. Think about the relief you felt when the storm ended. What lessons did you learn from those experiences that would apply to a storm you're currently facing? Take a moment right now to ask God to lead you safely through this storm to the other side.

A Content Heart (Chapter 7)

Ponder these questions:

- In what area of life have you recently been playing the "When-Then" game? Imagine that your "when" has come true. Now list all the other areas of life where you won't feel happy because the "when" hasn't occurred in those areas. List some ways you can find contentment in the present (such as thanking God for all your shoes!).
- Think of someone you know who seems genuinely content. What qualities does that person have that seem to be characteristic of contentment? How can you practice those traits?

Memorize 1 Timothy 6:6–8.

Take action: Make a list of the five things for which you're most grateful. For the next month, begin your prayer time thanking God for these five things He's given you.

A Serving Heart (Chapter 8)

Ponder these questions:

- If you wrote your epitaph, what would you want it to say today? If you worked at developing a serving heart—if you practiced serving God and others by putting their needs before your own—what would your epitaph say?
- In this chapter, you read Peggy Noonan's account of the crowds cheering construction laborers, public servants, and medical personnel in New York City in the aftermath of 9/11. What's the greatest example of servanthood you've ever seen? List the qualities you saw in the person who was serving. List the responses of the person being served. Who do you think benefited the most in that situation?

Memorize Philippians 2:3–5.

Take action: For each of the next four weeks, select one person for whom you'll make a genuine sacrifice of time or money in order to meet a practical need. Decide that you'll tell no one else about it.

A Praying Heart (Chapter 9)

Ponder these questions:

- Why don't we pray more? Which of these reasons most resonates with you?
    - You feel guilty about your prayerlessness.
    - It takes a titanic struggle to spend even five or ten minutes a day talking to God.
    - When your will does win out over your desires and you begin to pray, you find it difficult to concentrate.
    - Deep down you really wonder if, beyond the momentary relief you feel, prayer really makes any difference.
- Prayer is vital to keeping your relationship with God vibrant. Describe your current relationship with Him. What can you do to improve your relationship with God? What step(s) will you take to find time for intimate and honest sharing with Him?

Memorize Philippians 4:6–7.

Take action: Make a "Worry List" that details everything you're concerned about in your life. Now, transfer those items to your "Prayer List." Next to each request, record the date. Leave a space on the right-hand side of the page to record God's answers. Spend a few moments before you get out of bed in the morning and before you drift off to sleep at night using this list as a guide to tell God about your concerns.

Beginning the Process

"Spiritual transformation is more than a to-do list to be checked off," some might argue. I agree. But such complaints remind me of the story of the person who reportedly said to evangelist D. L. Moody, "Your method of evangelism is too simple." "Maybe it is," Moody responded, "but I like my way of sharing the gospel better than your way of not sharing it."

The suggestions I've made for beginning the process of transforming your heart are just that—a beginning. But to be intentional about this subject of spiritual transformation, we need to start somewhere.

Almost two hundred pages ago, at the beginning of chapter 1, I asked you to imagine moving to an unfamiliar city. How would you prepare for such a relocation, especially if you knew you'd never return to where you are living now? How much energy would you devote to accumulating money, acquiring possessions, or attaining a promotion in your present situation if you couldn't take any of those things with you to your new location?

As I told you all those pages ago, you *are* going to make such a move one day. The departure date is already fixed on God's calendar and—although it's unknown to you—it's even closer now than it was when you began reading this book. When moving day arrives, you'll be forced to leave everything behind. Even that body of yours that you have spent so much energy, money, and time maintaining will be left to decompose in a grave. All you'll take with you on departure day is the heart you've developed.

And are you so pleased with the condition of your heart—with the sum total of your thoughts, desires, and decisions—that you'd like to spend eternity with it just as it is? How do you think God would evaluate the condition of your heart at this moment in time?

Doctors say, "Take care of your body; it's the only one you get." God says, "Watch over your heart with all diligence" (Proverbs 4:23) because it's the only part of you that's eternal.

Such a realization is the best reason I know to begin the process of spiritual transformation *now*.

Clutter-Free Christianity
Robert Jeffress

Chapter 1: The Heart of the Matter

1. If you knew that in six months you were going to die and come face to face with God, what changes would you make in your life? Why?

2. Can Christians do anything to please God? Why or why not?

3. The author mentions "correct theology" and "embracing the right cultural causes" as substitutes for the essence of Christianity. Do you agree that this is happening today? Why or why not? What other secondary concerns, if any, have cluttered Christianity and distracted us from the essence of our faith?

4. In Luke 10:27, Jesus reduced all of God's laws to two: love God with all your heart and love others as yourself. On a scale of 1–10, with 10 being the best, grade yourself on how well you keep each of these commands. Which one is more difficult for you to fulfill? Why?

Chapter 2: Simply Supernatural

1. Why do you think the subject of spiritual transformation fails to excite many Christians?

2. Define what you think Paul meant in Romans 8:29 when he said that God's purpose is to conform us to the image of Christ.

3. Of the four reasons the author gives for failing to experience spiritual transformation—we don't feel it's necessary, we don't find the goal desirable, we don't think it's possible, we haven't planned for it—with which do you most identify? What can you do to eliminate that particular excuse?

4. Do you have an intentional plan for becoming more like Christ? Why or why not? What are the essential ingredients for an intentional pursuit of Christlikeness?

Chapter 3: Heart Surgery

1. How would you explain the concept of the kingdom of God to someone? How has this chapter changed your concept of God's kingdom?

2. What is the danger of limiting the kingdom of God to the next life? What is the danger of limiting it to this world only? To which extreme do the Christians you know gravitate? Why do you think that's the case?

3. Why do you think many Christians fail to understand the role they must play in their own spiritual transformation? Do you agree with the author that spiritual transformation is a joint project involving God's power and our effort? Why or why not?

4. The author mentions three essential components to the process of spiritual transformation. Of these three—the desire, a plan, and the discipline—which one is the most lacking in your life? Identify one or two things you can do to change that.

Chapter 4: A Forgiving Heart

1. How would you define *forgiveness*?

2. Do you agree with the author's contention that Christians struggle as much with forgiveness as non-Christians? Why do you think we have such a difficult time forgiving others?

3. Is it possible to forgive someone, yet choose to not reestablish a relationship with that person? Why or why not?

4. Read Matthew 6:14–15. Is Jesus saying that a Christian can lose salvation if he or she refuses to forgive? If not, what is He saying?

Chapter 5: An Obeying Heart

1. How would you explain the difference between obedience (which Jesus commended) and legalism (which Jesus condemned)?

2. The author mentions three characteristics of the kind of obedience God desires from us: immediate obedience, complete obedience, and joyful obedience. Which characteristic do you think is most important to God? Why?

3. Of the two barriers that make obedience to God difficult—distance and distrust—with which do you most struggle? Why?

4. Is the anticipation of a future reward from God a proper motivation for obedience? Why or why not? Defend your answer from Scripture.

Chapter 6: A Trusting Heart

1. How would you define *faith*? Why do you think the Bible places such a premium on faith?

2. If someone were to come to you expressing great doubt that God could ever forgive him or her, what would you say? What one passage of Scripture would you use to demonstrate the power of God's love?

3. Why do you think Christians who have no difficulty believing in God's power to create the universe often struggle with trusting in His power over their life circumstances?

4. The author contends that "God knows what lies ahead of you, because He has planned what lies ahead of you." Do you agree with his statement? Why or why not? What comfort do you find in that truth? Explain.

Chapter 7: A Content Heart

1. In what specific area of your life do you struggle with contentment? Why do you think that is?

2. Complete this sentence: "Once I have _____, then I will be content." What is the fallacy of such a belief?

3. With whom do you tend to compare yourself? What in that person's life do you most desire? Can comparison to another person ever be helpful? Under what circumstances?

4. Suppose your child has a C average in school but says, "I'm content with my grade point average"? How would you respond? What's the difference between contentment and laziness?

Chapter 8: A Serving Heart

1. Write an epitaph for yourself by which you would like to be remembered by your friends and family.

2. What aspect of servanthood do most people misunderstand? Why? How does Jesus's example of servanthood correct that misunderstanding?

3. Think about an instance in your life when you gave up something important for the benefit of someone else. How did you

feel immediately after making that sacrifice? Six months later, did you feel better or worse about your choice?

4. What new insight about servanthood did you gain from reading this chapter?

Chapter 9: A Praying Heart

1. Why do you think Christians find it difficult to make time to pray?

2. How would you answer someone who said, "Why pray if God is sovereign and has already determined what is going to happen?"

3. Does the length of our prayers matter to God? Why or why not? Is there a difference between the length of our prayers and the amount of time we devote to prayer? If so, explain the difference.

4. What one insight about prayer can you immediately put into practice to develop more of a praying heart?

Chapter 10: The Transformed Heart

1. If God were to take a snapshot of your heart right now, what would be His evaluation of its condition? What things about your heart would please God? What aspects of your heart would displease Him?

2. What is the primary wrong assumption that keeps Christians from experiencing spiritual transformation in their lives? How has your attitude about spiritual transformation changed as a result of your reading this book?

3. Throughout this book the author has described numerous benefits of allowing God to rule over every aspect of your life. Which of these benefits is most appealing to you? Why?

4. At the end of this chapter, the author suggests an intentional plan to help you develop the kind of heart God desires. We invite you to spend the next two months concentrating on each of these qualities, one by one, so that you can experience the supernatural existence God desires for you.

Notes

Chapter 1

1. Dallas Willard, *Renovation of the Heart: Putting on the Character of Christ* (Colorado Springs: NavPress, 2002), 14.
2. Hans Hofmann, quoted in Thom S. Rainer and Eric Geiger, *Simple Church: Returning to God's Process for Making Disciples* (Nashville: Broadman & Holman, 2006), 57.

Chapter 2

1. Dallas Willard, *Renovation of the Heart: Putting on the Character of Christ* (Colorado Springs: NavPress, 2002), 57.

Chapter 3

1. Mark Buchanan, *Your God Is Too Safe: Rediscovering the Wonder of a God You Can't Control* (Sisters, OR: Multnomah, 2001), 133.
2. Elton Trueblood, *The Company of the Committed* (New York: Harper & Brothers, 1961), 41, quoted in Gordon MacDonald, *A Resilient Life: You Can Move Ahead No Matter What* (Nashville: Nelson, 2004), 151.

Chapter 4

1. John Ortberg, *Everybody's Normal Till You Get to Know Them* (Grand Rapids: Zondervan, 2003), 165.
2. C. S. Lewis, *Mere Christianity* (San Francisco: HarperCollins, 2001), 115.
3. Jeff Jacoby, "Undeserved Forgiveness," *Boston Globe,* October 8, 2006, quoted in Stan Guthrie, "The Scandal of Forgiveness," *Christianity Today* 51, no. 1 (January 2007): 58.

4. Anne Lamott, *Traveling Mercies: Some Thoughts on Faith* (New York: Pantheon, 1999), 128, 134, quoted in John Ortberg, *Everybody's Normal*, 166.

5. Lewis Smedes, *Shame and Grace: Healing the Shame We Don't Deserve* (New York: HarperCollins, 1993), 136, 141, quoted in Philip Yancey, *What's So Amazing About Grace?* (Grand Rapids: Zondervan, 1997), 99–100.

6. George Herbert, quoted in Yancey, *What's So Amazing About Grace?*, 82.

7. "Beaten Woman Says Attack a 'Blessing,'" *Dallas Morning News*, January 13, 2007.

8. Charles R. Swindoll, *Hope Again* (Dallas: Word, 1996), 188.

Chapter 5

1. W. E. Vine, *Vine's Expository Dictionary of New Testament Words* (Old Tappan, NJ: Revell, 1966), 124, quoted in John F. MacArthur Jr., *The Gospel According to Jesus: What Does Jesus Mean When He Says, "Follow Me"?* (Grand Rapids: Zondervan, 1988), 174.

2. Haddon Robinson, quoted in Philip Yancey, *Prayer: Does It Make Any Difference?* (Grand Rapids: Zondervan, 2006), 86–87.

3. John Piper, *The Supremacy of God in Preaching* (Grand Rapids: Baker, 1990), 24–25.

4. William Law, *A Serious Call to a Devout and Holy Life: The Spirit of Love* (New York: Paulist, 1978), 57, quoted in Dallas Willard, *The Divine Conspiracy: Rediscovering Our Hidden Life in God* (New York: HarperCollins, 1998), 298.

5. Frank C. Laubach, *Letters by a Modern Mystic* (Westwood: Fleming H. Revell, 1937), 17, quoted in John Ortberg, *The Life You've Always Wanted: Spiritual Disciplines for Ordinary People* (Grand Rapids: Zondervan, 1997), 147.

6. Oswald Chambers, quoted in John Eldredge, *Wild at Heart: Discovering the Passionate Soul of a Man* (Nashville: Nelson, 2001), 219.

7. Philip Yancey, *Reaching for the Invisible God: What Can We Expect to Find?* (Grand Rapids: Zondervan, 2000), 90–91.

Chapter 6

1. Alan Redpath, quoted in David Jeremiah, *A Bend in the Road* (Nashville: Word, 2000), 33.

2. M. Scott Peck, *The Road Less Traveled: A New Psychology of Love, Traditional Values and Spiritual Growth* (New York: Simon & Schuster, 1978), 16.

3. Henri J. M. Nouwen, *Sabbatical Journey: The Diary of His Final Year* (New York: Crossroad, 1998), viii. From the preface, quoted in John Ortberg, *If You Want to Walk on Water, You've Got to Get Out of the Boat* (Grand Rapids: Zondervan, 2001), 182.

Chapter 7

1. Harold Kushner, *When All You've Ever Wanted Isn't Enough* (New York: Simon & Schuster, 1986), 146.

2. Patrick M. Morley, *The Seven Seasons of a Man's Life: Examining the Unique Challenges Men Face* (Nashville: Nelson, 1995), 20.

3. John Piper, *Brothers, We Are Not Professionals: A Plea to Pastors for Radical Ministry* (Nashville: Broadman & Holman, 2002), 45.

4. Mark Buchanan, *The Holy Wild* (Sisters, OR: Multnomah, 2003), 106–7.

5. Robert J. Hastings, "The Station," quoted in Robert Jeffress, *The Road Most Traveled: Releasing the Power of Contentment in Your Life* (Nashville: Broadman & Holman, 1996), 6–7.

Chapter 8

1. Dorothy L. Sayers, *Christian Letters to a Post-Christian World: A Selection of Essays* (Grand Rapids: Eerdmans, 1969), 14. Quoted in Philip Yancey, *Where Is God When It Hurts?* (Grand Rapids: Zondervan, 1977), 161–62.

2. Peggy Noonan, "Welcome Back, Duke," *Wall Street Journal,* October 12, 2001.

Chapter 9

1. Philip Yancey, *Prayer: Does It Make Any Difference?* (Grand Rapids: Zondervan, 2006), 13–14.

2. Oswald Chambers, *Prayer: A Holy Occupation* (Grand Rapids: Discovery House, 1992), 97.

3. Ben Patterson, *Deepening Your Conversation with God: Learning to Love to Pray* (Minneapolis: Bethany House, 1999, 2001), 118–19.

4. Friedrich Heiler, *Prayer: A Study in the History and Psychology of Religion* (London: Oxford University Press, 1932), 89. Quoted in Yancey, *Prayer*, 131.

5. Walter Wink, "Prayer and the Powers: History Belongs to the Intercessors," *Sojourners,* October 1990, 14, quoted in Yancey, *Prayer,* 130.

6. Andrew Murray, quoted in Yancey, *Prayer,* 131.

7. John Piper, *Brothers, We Are Not Professionals: A Plea to Pastors for Radical Ministry* (Nashville: Broadman & Holman, 2002), 53.

8. Richard J. Foster, *Devotional Classics* (New York: Harper, 1990, 1991, 1993), 137, quoted in Charles Swindoll, *So, You Want to Be Like Christ? Eight Essentials to Get You There* (Nashville: W Publishing Group, 2005), 120.

9. C. S. Lewis, *Mere Christianity* (San Francisco: HarperCollins, 2001), 198.

10. Thomas R. Kelly, *A Testament of Devotion* (New York: Harper & Brothers, 1941), 35, quoted in John Ortberg, *The Life You've Always Wanted: Spiritual Disciplines for Ordinary People* (Grand Rapids: Zondervan, 1997), 143.

Chapter 10

1. C. S. Lewis, "Meditation in a Toolshed," in *God in the Dock: Essays on Theology and Ethics.* ed. Walter Hooper (Grand Rapids: Eerdmans, 1973), 212, quoted in Philip Yancey, *Disappointment with God: Three Questions No One Asks Aloud* (Grand Rapids: Zondervan, 1988), 218.

2. Oswald Chambers, *The Psychology of Redemption* (London: Marshall, Morgan & Scott, 1955), 26–27, quoted in Dallas Willard, *The Spirit of the Disciplines: Understanding How God Changes Lives* (San Francisco: Harper, 1988), 118.

3. Philip Yancey, *Prayer: Does It Make Any Difference?* (Grand Rapids: Zondervan, 2006), 103.

Robert Jeffress is pastor of the legendary 10,800-member First Baptist Church in Dallas. He previously served as senior pastor of the 9,500-member First Baptist Church of Wichita Falls, Texas.

Dr. Jeffress is a magna cum laude graduate of Baylor University with a bachelor of arts in business and communications. He earned a master of theology degree from Dallas Theological Seminary and a doctor of ministry degree from Southwestern Baptist Theological Seminary.

He is the author of more than sixteen books, including the bestsellers *The Solomon Secrets* and *Outrageous Truth* (previously published as *Hell? Yes!*). He hosts the First Baptist Dallas television programs on the 316 Network, which includes weekly Bible teaching broadcasts on television, radio, and the Internet, which can be viewed and heard at www.firstdallas.org. He is also the teacher on the internationally broadcast program *Pathway to Victory*.

Dr. Jeffress's wife, Amy, is a graduate of the University of Texas at Austin and Tarleton State University; they have two daughters.

If your soul is thirsty for a deeper, more meaningful relationship with Christ, reach for these titles by Dr. Jeffress!

Using the Bible story of the prodigal son as a backdrop, *Coming Home* explains how you can return to a vibrant relationship with God.

I Want More! is a refreshing, Bible-based book designed to help you satisfy your spiritual hunger for more of the Holy Spirit.

God's wisdom, articulated by Solomon as "uncommon sense for extraordinary success," holds the key to achieving and enjoying the things we want most in life.

Second Chance, Second Act will show you how to use your mistakes as a prelude to a fresh start in life.

WATERBROOK PRESS
www.waterbrookpress.com

The Essential Tools You Need to Defend Your Faith, Recognize God's Role in Suffering, and Break Free from the Past.

In *Outrageous Truth,* Dr. Jeffress issues a bold wake-up call to all believers—from college students to grandparents—to stop apologizing for and start proclaiming the tough but essential truths that Christians have historically embraced.

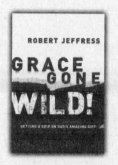

Grace Gone Wild! challenges you to gain a biblical understanding of grace, and reveals how "good grace" can protect your marriage, church, and relationships from abuse.

This powerful book reveals the war Satan is waging against followers of Christ and gives you six strategies for defeating Satan's destructive plan—and living victoriously in God's unshakable power.

In *When Forgiveness Doesn't Make Sense,* Robert Jeffress lays bare the cancerous tumor of unforgiveness and walks you through the confusing and sometimes thorny path to peace.

WATERBROOK PRESS
www.waterbrookpress.com